INSTRUCTOR'S MANUAL

to accompany

Faigley/Selzer
GOOD REASONS WITH CONTEMPORARY ARGUMENTS
Fourth Edition

Matthew Newcomb
Pennsylvania State University

Revised by

John Jones
University of Texas at Austin

New York Boston San Francisco
London Toronto Sydney Tokyo Singapore Madrid
Mexico City Munich Paris Cape Town Hong Kong Montreal

Instructor's Manual to accompany Faigley/Selzer, *Good Reasons with Contemporary Arguments, Fourth Edition*

Copyright ©2009 Pearson Education, Inc.

ISBN: 0-205-61685-2

2 3 4 5 6 7 8 9 10–OPM–11 10 09 08

CONTENTS

Part 4: Designing and Presenting Arguments

Part 5: Researching Arguments

Part 6: Contemporary Arguments

v

Preface

The aim of this book is to help you use *Good Reasons with Contemporary Arguments* effectively in teaching your course in rhetoric and composition. The Preface of *Good Reasons with Contemporary Arguments* offers a brief introduction to the textbook for you and your students. The distinctive features of the book are:

- Its fundamental conviction that courses in rhetoric and composition teach skills to students that they will need not only in school but also in the workplace and as citizens of a participatory democracy.

- Its refusal to make the distinctions central to so many other textbooks of this type. In *Good Reasons with Contemporary Arguments*, Faigley and Selzer are not concerned with classifying certain arguments as "rational" and others as "irrational," nor do they try to draw a line between "argument" and "persuasion." They also do not teach Stephen Toulmin's method of analyzing arguments. It is their opinion that the Toulmin method and the aforesaid distinctions often obscure the central goal of an argument: to convince a particular audience of a given claim by using effective logical, ethical, and pathetic appeals.

- Its emphasis both on the structure and content of arguments, and on their delivery and presentation.

Here we'll say a few further words about these features of the book, and make a few suggestions about using both *Good Reasons with Contemporary Arguments* and this instructor's manual in your course.

Why Students Find Courses in Rhetoric and Composition Challenging

Even though many students can write about their own lives with skill and ease when they get to college, very few can write effective arguments. Writing a strong, persuasive argument is difficult work. To do so requires a range of skills—from assessing the needs of an audience and finding good reasons that address those needs, to formatting your work in a manner appropriate to its particular rhetorical situation. Mastering these many different skills takes time and experience. Throughout your course, many of your students' questions will be what we might call "skill questions." How can I write an analysis of this article without making it sound like a simple summary? What counts as good evidence? Can I ever use "I" in writing college essays? How do I cite an online magazine article according to MLA style?

Writing strong, effective arguments, however, requires more than simply a set of skills. We've noticed that, in courses like the one you are teaching, students often struggle with writing assignments because the assignments require that the students think of writing not *primarily* as a form of self-expression. Instead of talking about themselves—and being true to their own imagination and experience—they are required to think of an audience and its needs, expectations, and values. Perhaps for the first time in their lives, they have to imagine in their writing the needs of an audience larger than themselves (and their teachers) and shape their work accordingly.

How to Use this Instructor's Manual

In the first half of this manual, we offer further discussion of the material presented in this fourth edition of *Good Reasons with Contemporary Arguments*. For each chapter, we offer a brief discussion of that chapter's content and then provide suggestions for in-class activities (including discussions) and short assignments related to the content of that chapter. This edition of *Good Reasons with Contemporary Arguments* has added new information boxes, titled "Finding Good Reasons." Additional ideas for including the material in these boxes in your course can be found in the in-class activities and short assignment sections of this manual. Although the chapter discussions sometimes build on each other, they are designed to be self-contained, so you can address the chapters in any order you choose in your class.

We also provide discussion questions for each reading selection in *Good Reasons with Contemporary Arguments*. You'll note that, for each selection, the first few questions are more or less the same. We ask students to identify the central claims of each reading, the author's argumentative purpose, and the reasons the author supplies to support his or her central claims.

Repeating these questions as frequently as possible reminds students of the focus of the course and trains them to look for claims and good reasons when they read.

In the second half of this manual, we provide model assignments and several plans for semester syllabi based on *Good Reasons with Contemporary Arguments*. While this collection of materials reflects our own particular pedagogical philosophy and idiosyncrasies, we hope that if you don't find them useful, you'll at least find them a helpful model to work against.

Finally, unless otherwise noted, all specific examples from outside images and texts that are mentioned in this manual—such as the short stories listed on p. 51—were freely available online at the time of this writing.

We wish you a very rewarding teaching experience with the fourth editions of *Good Reasons with Contemporary Arguments* and the *Instructor's Manual*.

Introduction: Persuading with Good Reasons

The primary goals of the introduction to *Good Reasons with Contemporary Arguments* are to expand your students' understanding of the term *argument* and to provide some basic guidelines for respectful, written arguments. Arguments, they might think, are disagreements—and, therefore, disagreeable. Arguments are about yelling and fighting, opposition and division. Your students might assume that in an argument the supporters on one side of an issue are more concerned with advancing their own position than they are with learning or with being receptive to the other side of the issue. Of course, this may be an exaggeration of your students' understanding of arguments; however, it is crucial that you discuss with your students the more charitable definitions of *argument* that are found in this section of the text in your first few class meetings.

You may find it helpful to go through the characteristics of written arguments and the guidelines for arguing respectfully as a group in one of these early class meetings and to return to these lists periodically throughout the semester.

IN-CLASS ACTIVITIES

• Give the students a brief overview of the introduction to *Good Reasons with Contemporary Arguments*, and try to develop a provisional definition of "argument," one that you can revise later in the term. Urge students to develop a definition flexible enough to allow for all attempts at persuasion. Ask your students what makes a particular argument effective. How, for instance, does an effective argument relate to the given audience? Does it appeal to the audience's sense of reason only, or does it also affect their emotions? What about the person making the argument? Does he or she matter? Does the situation in which the argument is being made matter?

• Have students describe in 1–2 detailed paragraphs a speech or essay that they found particularly persuasive or memorable, focusing on the qualities that made it compelling to them. Have them present these qualities to the rest of the class and collect them in some central place for later access. You can do this by writing unique qualities on the board and having students copy them in their notes, or by electing one student to take notes of the discussion and post those notes to a course Web site or blog. You can then use these qualities to ground your discussion of early course readings until students are introduced to the rhetorical terminology in *Good Reasons*.

• Have your students hold on to the previous exercise. In the second half of the course, have them rewrite it using the technical vocabulary they have encountered in *Good Reasons*.

SHORT ASSIGNMENTS

• Have students make a list of *all* the arguments that they encounter on any given day. The responses will range from advertisements and editorials, to essays written for other courses and discussions with their roommates about the quality of cafeteria food. Encourage students to think creatively. Is a tote bag printed with the name of an organic grocery a kind of argument? Does it make only one argument, or more than one? Are fashion styles kinds of argument? If so, what claim does a person make about him- or herself by wearing, say, a particular brand of jeans? In class, when you discuss several students' lists, make sure you address the varied ways in which arguments are made. How does the argument of a five-page essay differ from, say, that of the latest advertisement for an energy drink? Each is an act of persuasion, but each makes its case in a way that is distinct from the other.

Part 1: Reading and Discovering Arguments

Chapter 1: Why Argue?

This chapter is a case study of the development of and reaction to Rachel Carson's book *Silent Spring*. Faigley and Selzer use this in-depth account of the author and her book to introduce key terms and concepts important to reading and writing arguments: the author's audience and that audience's importance to the kinds of arguments that he or she makes; the goals of argumentation and the existence of different types of arguments, like position and proposal arguments, that can satisfy these goals; and the rhetorical appeals, ethos, pathos, and logos.

Many students will have no trouble understanding these rhetorical concepts. What they will struggle with, however, is putting this understanding into practice by creating and analyzing arguments. Thus, you may want to reassure your students that, while the concepts discussed in *Good Reasons with Contemporary Arguments* are not intellectually challenging, what is difficult, and what they will spend the entire term working on, is their practical application.

Finally, when discussing this chapter with your students, it may be helpful to begin to dispel some of the myths about writing that many of them hold, either consciously or unconsciously. The first of these is the myth that good writers "just write" well. During the course of this discussion, emphasize that, while some good writing is the result of inspiration, writing is most often a deliberate task that primarily depends on the author making specific choices about the kinds of techniques he or she will use in a specific situation. You may then want to tell your students that the course will introduce them to a variety of critical and argumentative tools that will enable them to improve their reading and writing skills by allowing them to make informed decisions about what techniques they can use to make their own arguments more effective.

Analyzing Arguments: Pathos, Ethos, *and* Logos

In *Good Reasons with Contemporary Arguments*, Faigley and Selzer re-iterate Aristotle's point: pathetic, ethical, and logical appeals are the three primary means of *making one's argument*. Explain to your students that they will encounter these appeals throughout the next few chapters. Here, you are simply introducing them to these concepts, and they should recognize that an argument's persuasiveness in its particular rhetorical context is not solely determined by its claims and reasons. The person making the argument is also important. Does he or she seem credible? Is the audience already familiar with him or her? Why, you might ask, do companies scramble to sign Venus Williams and Tiger Woods to endorse sports-related paraphernalia? (A more difficult question: why do other companies have them endorse non-sports related paraphernalia?) The skill with which the writer or speaker addresses the values of his or her audience is also crucial to determining that argument's effectiveness. Remind students of the ads of charity and relief agencies: what does an ad for an animal shelter generally feature? How about an ad for famine relief? What arguments do these advertisements make, and how do they make them?

Also emphasize to your students that pathetic, ethical, and logical appeals often overlap. An ethical appeal can simultaneously be a pathetic appeal, and *vice versa*. A "because" clause, which is generally part of the logical structure of an argument, can appeal strongly to the values or emotions of the audience: "Vote for Ralph Nader because he supports the protection of the environment." Therefore, emphasize to your students that what one person may understand and discuss primarily in terms of a pathetic appeal, another may understand and discuss primarily in terms of a logical appeal. Also emphasize that many times, the author of a given text will rely more heavily on one or more of the appeals than on the others.

Most students find *pathos, ethos,* and *logos* powerful tools for analysis. These concepts are dealt with more fully in the introduction to rhetorical analysis in Chapter 5 of *Good Reasons with Contemporary Arguments*. Even though Chapters 8–13 of *Good Reasons with Contemporary Arguments* require students to recognize and practice other argumentative strategies, you may want to reiterate the importance of pathos, ethos, and logos when you introduce your students to these other kinds of argument, since rhetoricians consider these appeals the cornerstone of all argumentation.

Position and Proposal Arguments

At this early stage in the term or semester, you don't want to overwhelm students with too many concepts or terms. However, if you plan to assign a proposal argument later in the course, you may want to spend some time going over the distinctions between position and proposal arguments. Briefly introduce to your students the types of arguments they will be learning about and practicing: definitional, causal, evaluative, narrative, rebuttal, and proposal arguments.

CARSON, "THE OBLIGATION TO ENDURE"

Use Carson's chapter as a way of introducing critical reading strategies, including the critical reading tool of rhetorical analysis.

1. What is Carson's central claim? What reasons and evidence does she provide to support this claim? What is her purpose in making her argument?
2. In what ways does Carson establish herself as a credible voice in this debate? In what ways does she reach out to the emotions and values of her audience? To the standards of logic and reason?
3. How does the structure of this chapter—the way that Carson organizes the content of the chapter—evidence Carson's awareness of her audience?

IN-CLASS ACTIVITIES

• Similar to the discussion of *argument* in the introduction, you will need to ask your students early in the semester what they understand the term *rhetoric* to mean. (Note: You might find it useful to combine this discussion with that discussion of argument.) Do your students define rhetoric as meaningless speechifying? Come to some consensus regarding the definition that you will use in your course.

• *Finding Good Reasons: Who's Using Up Earth's Resources?* Have your students bring to class other maps, similar to the ecological footprint map, and share them with the class. (These maps could be ones the students create themselves using the annotation features of Google Maps or other mapping programs.) Discuss the kinds of arguments these maps make. What reasons are implicit in the design?

• One of Faigley and Selzer's key arguments in *Good Reasons with Contemporary Arguments* is that writers make arguments in order to bring about changes in society. Perhaps you will want to apply this claim to the rhetorical purposes of arguments. Some arguments are intended to persuade an audience to accept a particular opinion or set of premises. Some arguments are crafted primarily to inform. Some arguments seem crafted as explorations, others as exercises in extending a particular thought or faith. Compare an editorial from a newspaper, an advertisement for an SUV, and the lyrics of a popular song. Ask the students what is the purpose of each. After collecting their answers, ask the more difficult question: How can the purposes be determined from a text when they are not specifically stated by the author(s)?

• Develop a handout with questions asking students about their reading practices. When do they do most of their course reading? Do they read with pen or pencil in hand? Do they read things straight through, incrementally, or in fits and starts? Do they try to get an overview before plowing right in? Do they ever experience a sense of disorientation when beginning a reading assignment or feel that they are not absorbing the content of the print? These are important questions. By asking them, your goal is to encourage students to become savvy, self-aware readers. Explain that *experienced* readers often don't begin by reading a given text from beginning to end or in the order of the page numbers. Scholars, for instance, often read an article's introduction, conclusion, and bibliography before reading it straight through, while CEOs read the executive summary and then flip to the conclusion. Emphasize that students have the power to skip around when they read. By getting a general sense of an article—by reading the opening and closing statements and all the subheads, for instance—they will be better able to read the piece critically and carefully. You might model for students how you read newspaper editorials or scholarly articles in your field, just to show them how one experienced reader goes about his or her work. Finally, you might also emphasize that it is difficult and disorienting to read effectively if you don't know much about a text's rhetorical context. Assure them this disorientation is normal, and will go away as they learn more about the topic.

• Place your students in groups of 3–4, and ask them to construct a brief *position* argument that follows the model given in this chapter. Then choose one of the arguments that the students have prepared and discuss it with the entire class. Ask the students who prepared the argument which of the first two components of the argument they had the most difficulty preparing: defining the issue, or taking a clear position on the issue? Ask the other students to offer suggestions on how they would improve the third component, offering reasons and evidence and acknowledging opposition views.

• Repeat the previous assignment with *proposal* arguments. Again, choose one of the proposal arguments that the students have prepared and discuss with the whole class. Do the other students agree that the problem is in fact a problem? Can they add to or revise the solution or solutions that have been given to correct the problem?

• Ask students what topics they know a lot about. In what fields could they use their expertise to encourage change, or make position arguments and proposal arguments? Students, of course, are not limited to those subjects in which they have special knowledge, but remind them that special knowledge is a good indicator of authentic interest. Rachel Carson, for instance, knew a great deal about biology and ecology, and this knowledge had everything to do with her passionate concern for the natural environment. Ask your students how effective *Silent Spring* would have been if Carson had not had this expertise.

SHORT ASSIGNMENTS

• To provide more practice in critical reading, have your students find one or several texts on their own (from the campus newspaper or a magazine, perhaps) and have them answer the questions about Carson's essay for the texts they have chosen. For each text, the student should identify the text's intended audience(s), the specific context(s) in which the argument is being made, and the author's purpose in making the argument.

• Have students read a piece of persuasive writing and highlight (directly in the text) every pathetic, ethical, and logical appeal employed by the author. Then, have students very briefly summarize and assess the author's use of each appeal (in a paragraph or so). Students should consider, for instance, how the author sought to employ emotional appeals in the text and whether that strategy was appropriate to this particular situation. (This assignment prepares students to write a rhetorical analysis, which is discussed in Chapter 5 of *Good Reasons with Contemporary Arguments*.) (Note: if your students all read the same text, you will likely find that some students have identified the same passage as using different logical appeals. Additionally, some students may find it difficult to ascribe just one appeal to a particular section of the text. Use these reactions to emphasize the interdependence of these appeals, such as the ways in which the author's use of pathetic or logical appeals affects the reader's perception—or the ethos—of that author.)

Chapter 2: Reading Arguments

Students should be aware early in the semester that some college writing assignments not only ask them to compose an effective argument but also to analyze the effectiveness of someone else's argument. For example, rhetorical analyses and evaluations are just such assignments. You will want to emphasize, therefore, that this course teaches students not only how to "write" arguments but also how to "read" arguments.

Another myth you may have to dispel for your students is that critical reading is not a skill. They might see it as something that some students are "naturally" better at than others. Therefore, make sure to emphasize to your students that critical reading is something all students can learn to master and that different texts require different methods of reading. While mastering critical reading does take some time and require some training, it is well within their reach.

In reviewing the material from this chapter, one effective means of communicating the connection between writing and reading to your students is to demonstrate how critical reading will often require them to begin "writing"—by annotating the text they are reading, or creating a summary or idea map of its contents—before they begin drafting their papers.

It might also be helpful to build on the discussion of writing on the Internet contained in the "Finding Good Reasons" box in this chapter. You may want to have your students compose blog entries during the course of the semester or use a blog for collecting their course notes and pre-writing exercises in place of a journal. It is often difficult to enact public writing in the rhetoric and composition classroom because the writing produced there usually stays there. However, by integrating blogs, podcasting, and online video with your course, you can give your students practice in writing for a wider audience.

IN-CLASS ACTIVITIES

• To supplement the examples given in the chapter, you may want to bring in an example of a text that you have annotated while reading. Students sometimes feel a holy reverence toward the printed word, one that has been inculcated in them through years of reading other people's books, such as library books and textbooks borrowed from their school. After showing them a text you have marked up, have them practice annotating a chapter from *Good Reasons with Contemporary Arguments*, then have a few volunteers share their annotations with the class, explaining why they marked what they did.

• *Finding Good Reasons: Has the Internet Made Everyone Writers?* With your students, look beyond blogs to other kinds of Internet writing. Apply the questions in this info box to product reviews on Amazon.com, videos posted on YouTube, or to information in MySpace or Facebook pages. What are the claims and reasons made by these texts or videos? How are they different from those made on blogs? How are they the same?

• Divide students into small groups, and have them create idea maps of a particular text. For this exercise, it would probably be best to have each group map a different text that is relevant to the entire class, such as chapters from *Good Reasons with Contemporary Arguments* or outside readings you have assigned (to conduct this exercise in class, you will most likely need to choose a text they have already read). When they are finished, have the groups briefly share their maps with the class. You may also want to provide permanent copies of the maps for each student to keep; you can do this by collecting the maps and making photocopies for each student. Or, if the technology is available to you, make digital copies of the maps (you or a student could take photographs of them with a digital camera or camera phone) and upload them to your course Web site or a free photo-sharing site where students can access them later.

SHORT ASSIGNMENTS

• Assign your students a text to summarize, either as individuals or in small groups. Choose a text that is relevant to the student: either one they will read as part of their regular course work, or one that they will use as research for a writing assignment in the course. (Note: If it is an outside reading, you will need to have students submit a copy of the text they are summarizing along with their summary, because it can be difficult to evaluate a summary of a text you haven't read.) Have them limit their summaries to one, single-spaced page. Since summarizing is a challenging skill for students to master, the first time students complete this assignment you will probably want to provide detailed annotations of their summaries, and then give them a chance to rewrite them.

• If your students are able to access the Internet reliably outside the classroom, such as in a campus computer lab, have them research free online tools for creating idea maps (which are also called "mind maps" or "flowcharts"). Have them make a list of 1–2 tools for creating these maps, and then briefly describe them: which is the easiest to use? Can the maps be printed or exported to other programs? Then have your students share these lists with each other in class or via your course Web site.

Chapter 3: Finding Arguments

This chapter functions as a general introduction to finding and recognizing good arguments. It also helps the student begin to be able to distinguish between statements that pose as arguments but are merely claims without reasons; between statements that pose as arguments but that are actually statements of fact, personal taste, or individual beliefs; and between arguments supported by good reasons and those that aren't.

Argument Structure

The *logical structure* of an argument consists of that argument's *central claim* and *reasons*.

What is a *claim*?

A claim is a proposition, assertion, opinion, or statement that some might consider a fact. Each of the following, for instance, is a claim:

- This soup is awful.

- The earth is round.

- *Barbershop* is the best movie ever made.

- We shouldn't put computers in classrooms.

- Martin stole my notebook.

Rarely are claims made as explicitly in the world as they are in academic papers, where the central claim of an essay usually sits right at the end of the opening paragraph. Remind students that the world is full of claims and that learning to recognize them is one of the primary skills involved in critical reading.

You might also remind your students that they have probably used other words in the past to identify claims. Reading an article they might have asked themselves, "What's the point here?" Reading a friend's essay they might have asked themselves, "Where's the thesis statement?" In both situations, they were looking for the central claim of the text before them. Explain, too, that we use the term claim in this course to emphasize the *arguable* nature of such statements. Claims that are arguable are assertions that are meant to be considered, challenged, defended with good reasons, and possibly revised. In short, a claim is not the final word on a topic, but, rather, it is often the beginning of a conversation about that topic.

What are *reasons*? What makes a *reason* a good reason?

Reasons are means of support that an author or audience can link to a claim. Good reasons are ones that the author or audience can accept as legitimate support for that claim. If your students struggle with our use of "link" here, explain that there is no one way to determine whether reasons are good reasons. You have to look at the claim and the rhetorical situation. Who's the audience? What's the occasion of the argument? What's the purpose of the person making the argument? Encourage them to use their own judgment when making the call.

What Is Not Arguable

"Arguability" is a crucial concept for students to understand. Students need to be consistently reminded that, when writing essays, their claims need to be *arguable* or controversial. According to Faigley and Selzer, claims are not arguable if they constitute a *fact,* an expression of *personal taste,* or a *belief* or *faith.* Of course, individuals, groups, institutions, and cultures have their own unique sense of what does and does not fit into these categories. Arguability, then, changes according to rhetorical context. Explore the implications of this point with your students. For example, most of us would not be interested in an essay arguing that child abuse is a crime, that Michael Jordan was a great basketball player, or that the events of September 11, 2001 were a tragedy. If the intended audience can easily respond, "yes, that is obvious" or "yes, that goes without saying" to the central claim, then the claim isn't arguable *for that audience.*

Additionally, you might also talk about the importance of understanding arguability in their academic or professional careers. Their success as students will be largely determined by their ability to produce, explore, and examine claims considered arguable in their chosen fields of study. Finally, you might consider reviewing the contents of this chapter when your students begin writing their own essays.

Finding and Exploring Topics

As you cover the material in this chapter on pre-writing—freewriting and brainstorming exercises, outlining—continue to emphasize for your students that writing is a process that consists of more than merely writing drafts of a final paper—or, as is typical of some students' process, writing a single draft of a final paper. Encourage them to experiment with these different pre-writing methods until they find the ones that they are most comfortable with and that are the most generative for them. You might have them regularly freewrite during the first five minutes of class, or encourage them to use the idea map tools they discovered in the short exercise from Chapter 2 (p. 17) to create outlines for their own papers. No matter how you choose to use these tools, it is crucial for you to assign and monitor your students' prewriting activities, for they will need to be comfortable with these activities when it is time for them to work on their major assignments.

Thinking about Audience

Students can struggle with the problem of audience when writing academic essays because they often associate this kind of writing with the writing they did in their high school literature classes. They assume that in your class they will be asked to write about the content of a particular text—its themes and meaning—and not about the kind of argument the author is making. Alternatively, they assume that the concepts and strategies you are interested in as a rhetoric teacher are the same concepts and strategies that English literature teachers are concerned with. Therefore, you might begin your discussion of audience by asking students about their past experiences with academic writing. You may find that many of your students will not be certain about what the term "audience" means. Ask them whom they're really writing for when they turn in their academic essays. How do they craft their work accordingly? Students may find that, in some instances, they already follow much of the advice that we offer in this chapter. In other instances, they will see that what English teachers appreciate and look for are not necessarily what other teachers or what other kinds of audiences appreciate and look for. Use this discussion of audience as a means of encouraging them to think more carefully and extensively about working within specific rhetorical situations.

While most of your students will never have to write for a rhetoric teacher again, and the audiences that they will be—and are currently—writing for elsewhere don't have the same concerns as you do, it is worthwhile for you to repeat throughout the semester that (depending on your assignments) you and their fellow classmates are the primary audience for the writing they will be doing in class. Therefore, you will be reading their essays not only for what the students are saying about a particular text or a particular social or political issue but for the type of argument they are making, whether a causal or proposal, evaluative or narrative. Therefore, the students should try to make as clear as possible when they write their papers that they are following the model for the given type of argument.

IN-CLASS ACTIVITIES

• *Finding Good Reasons: Are Traffic Cameras Invading Your Privacy?* Use the discussion of traffic cameras to spark a wider discussion of surveillance issues that are relevant to your students. For example, perhaps your state uses cameras to track speeders or wireless identification and high-speed photography at tollbooths, or maybe your university requires the use of swipe cards to control access to certain areas of campus. What happens to this information? Does it ever get used for purposes other than those they were designed for, such as tracking an individual's movements around campus or on the roads? Have your students brainstorm claims and reasons in response to these or other relevant surveillance issues.

• Have the students compare a short literary essay (for example, an analysis of a short story) to a newspaper editorial. What are the differences between the two texts with respect to the audience being addressed? Hopefully, comparisons such as this will help the students recognize that the approach to reading and writing that we use in *Good Reasons with Contemporary Arguments* is not limited to academic work or to certain kinds of academic work.

• Have the students work in groups of 4–5. Ask them to prepare a sample draft outline of a short argument that includes all four parts of a model argument. As outlined in Chapter 2, strong arguments typically consist of the following: i) an interesting *claim*; ii) at least one *good reason* that makes the claim worth making; iii) *evidence* for the reason(s); and iv) *opposing views* and admitted *limitations* of the argument.

• With regard to the section "Find Good Reasons," which introduces four main types of argument, distribute to the class a photocopy of two cartoons. Ask your students to define what a cartoon is (as opposed to other kinds of arguments that are both visual and verbal). (Chapter 8 provides Scott McCloud's definition of the cartoon. If any of your students have read that far, they can use that information.) Then ask your students to compare the two cartoons, state what is dissimilar and what is similar about their form (not content), and argue (or evaluate) which is the better cartoon.

• With regard to the section "Find Evidence to Support Good Reasons," emphasize to your students that good reasons are not enough to persuade. Most audiences require good evidence also. If your campus has a newspaper, find an editorial or an op-ed piece and assess its evidence. Ask the students if they consider the evidence *relevant* for the college community? Also, when discussing the issue of *relevant* evidence with students, deal both with kinds of evidence and with the potential sources of evidence. For example, asks the students what other kinds of evidence would be effective in writing such a piece or what sources of information would probably not provide relevant evidence for an article, say, on college students' taste in music?

• Also with regard to the section, "Find Evidence to Support Good Reasons," discuss the issue of *sufficient* evidence. Again, we suggest that you choose an editorial or an op-ed piece (perhaps the same piece that was used when you discussed the issue of *relevant* evidence). Is *enough* evidence provided to support each of the reasons? Has the writer chosen not to support some reasons with evidence? If so, does that detract from his or her persuasiveness? In what rhetorical situation might he or she have needed to use different kinds or amounts of evidence?

• You might encourage students to begin thinking about their own majors. What sources are well respected in their particular fields of study? What kinds of evidence will they need to learn to gather? It is possible that some of them will have chosen majors that require entire courses (with titles such as "statistics" and "research methods") in gathering, handling, and documenting information according to the conventions of their discipline.

• Ask your students to write down the definition for each fallacy listed in *Good Reasons with Contemporary Arguments* and then to provide a unique example of their own of that fallacy. The test functions as a diagnostic. It helps to assess which students are struggling to understand why the logical structure (a *claim* plus *reasons*) of an argument is weak. Afterwards, have each student swap his or her responses with someone else and then go through the answers together as a class.

• Another way to introduce the section "Fallacies in Arguments" to students is in the form of a game. Divide the class into groups of 4–6 students, depending on the size of the class. Each group writes up on the blackboard an example of one of the thirteen fallacies. Then the class comments on the answers. The exercise is a lot of fun for both the student and teacher. Students work on revising, or in some instances completely overhauling, the particular example of the given fallacy.

SHORT ASSIGNMENTS

• Have students (individually or in groups) choose a newspaper or magazine, examine it cover to cover, and write a profile of its audience based on its general content, advertisements, and design. This exercise is particularly interesting and effective if you have students choose a periodical from the past. By comparing, say, an 1895 issue of the *Atlantic Monthly* with an issue of *Garden and Forest* from the same year, students gain insight not only into the ways that a magazine's contents can suggest information about its readership but also into the history of American periodicals. (Note: A number of nineteenth-century periodicals are available online through the *Making of America* project [http://cdl.library.cornell.edu/moa/].)

• Have students develop a simple claim, such as "R.E.M. was the best band of the 1980s." Then ask the students to develop good reasons to support this claim in several different contexts, such as a campus paper, *Rolling Stone*, the *Wall Street Journal*, and a Web site devoted to "family values." (You might even have the students fabricate the evidence that they could use to support their reasons in each of these contexts.) The point of this assignment, of course, is to emphasize that no argument is made in isolation. A good reason in one context may be a bad one in another.

• The letters to the editor of your local or campus paper are often an impressive cache of logical fallacies (as are call-in radio shows and political debate programs such as "Crossfire"). Have your students read the letters (or listen to several radio shows, or watch several TV shows) over the period of a week. Ask them to find and identify as many logical fallacies as they possibly can. You might even make this a kind of scavenger hunt, and the student or team of students who compiles the longest and most varied list receives a treat. Alternatively, you might bring a photocopied article or taped program to class and ask the students to write down the fallacies they read or see in those verbal or visual texts.

Chapter 4: Drafting and Revising Arguments

It is likely that your students will have been told before about the importance of revision. However, try to *show* the students the centrality of revision to writing. As Faigley and Selzer note, it is important that you reiterate to your students that in order to revise effectively, first and foremost they need to give themselves enough time to revise. Students who complete essays 2–3 minutes before class deny themselves this opportunity. Second, emphasize to your students that they need to learn to prioritize the work involved in revising. *Good Reasons with Contemporary Arguments* offers extensive and detailed steps for the students to follow here. (The Revision Record assignment described later in this manual also emphasizes the importance of prioritizing the work done in the revision process.)

As a teacher, you can help students learn the lessons set forth by responding in a manner appropriate to the kind of work they've submitted. From experience, we find that line-editing a rough draft (and ignoring or giving short shrift to the student's claim and reasons) works against your attempts to teach writing as a skill that improves with practice. Thus, while you will want to emphasize the importance of sentence structure, word choice, and transitions between sentences, you don't want to ignore the larger argument your student is trying to make in order to prioritize these concerns. Discuss with other instructors effective means of responding to students' work, methods that make it clear that you have high standards but that also encourage your students to work on improving their writing.

Along these same lines, make sure that students connect the lessons of this chapter to their work as peer reviewers. Students often think that they provide effective responses to a paper written by one of their peers when they note sentence level errors such as a misspelled word, a pronoun referent disagreement, or an incorrect homonym. Remind the students to first read through the entire essay and figure out where the essay is in the process of composition before they offer advice to the author of the essay. Emphasize to them that when they offer advice, they need to offer assistance with the most important concerns, not the most minute.

IN-CLASS ACTIVITIES

• *Finding Good Reasons: Should Driving While Talking Be Banned?* Apply these questions to some driver-safety issue that is relevant to your students. For example, the prevalence of DVD players in some new cars, or the movements in some states to make 18 the minimum age to receive a driver's license.

• Save a piece of persuasive writing that students submitted to you and, after a week or so, return it to them unmarked in class. Have the students make a plan for its revision following the steps listed in the "Checklist for Evaluating Your Draft" in this chapter. Once students have completed their plans for revision, ask them if they now recognize ways of improving the essay that they *hadn't* been aware of before submitting it the first time. The point of this assignment, of course, is to provide students an opportunity they often don't provide themselves—namely, the opportunity to gain some distance from a piece of writing before revising it. You might then allow the students to revise the essay for homework and re-submit it for a grade.

• Find a student who is willing to share a selection of his or her writing with the rest of the class, preferably an early draft of a major assignment. After establishing the overall goals of the piece, work with the class on revising a few paragraphs of it as a group. If you have access to overhead projection, you can use it to share the text with your students. Otherwise, provide everyone with copies of the text. Try to allow your students to drive the revision process, but be sure to keep the focus of the activity on revising the meaning, structure, or arrangement of the selection, rather than just its surface features, like spelling and grammar. You can help alleviate some of the embarrassment that this kind of attention on student writing might cause by emphasizing that any problems found in the writing are going to be typical for students at their level, and keeping the tone of the exercise evaluative, rather than judgmental.

When choosing a text, it may be best to ask the student author for permission to use his or her writing privately so that he or she doesn't feel pressured to comply. You may also wish to present the text anonymously so as not to single out or embarrass the author. However, if you do so, still get the student's permission beforehand. Although some students may be initially reluctant to share their writing for this kind of exercise, often, once they recognize the benefits of group feedback, they will be more willing to volunteer if you use this exercise again.

SHORT ASSIGNMENTS

• Several instructors at The University of Texas have their students read 1–2 scholarly essays on student revision. Both Linda Flower, John Hayes, Linda Carey, Karen Schriver, and James Stratman's "Detection, Diagnosis, and the Strategies of Revision" (*College Composition* 37 [1986]: 16–55) and Jennie Nelson's "This Was an Easy Assignment: Examining How Students Interpret Academic Writing Tasks" (*Research in the Teaching of English* 24 [1990]: 362–396) are accessible articles that document the difference between what writing teachers expect of students in the revision process and what students often actually do when revising (you will likely need to acquire these essays through your library). You might consider having your students read one of these articles for homework and then discuss it with them in class. Or, you might summarize some of the article's findings and present them to students as a mini-lecture. In either case, instructors have found this activity an effective means of communicating to students what to do when revising.

Part 2: Analyzing Arguments

Chapter 5: Analyzing Written Arguments

The central points of this chapter are that the term *rhetoric* refers to both making good arguments as a writer and understanding good arguments as a reader, and that skill in the one activity improves skill in the other. The chapter summarizes two kinds of rhetorical analysis: *textual* analysis and *contextual* analysis. It also makes clear that these two kinds of analysis are not mutually exclusive, but that both are commonly found in analytical texts.

Textual Analysis

Point out to your students that the material in this chapter expands on the material in Chapter 1 that deals with analyzing arguments according to the appeals of ethos, pathos, and logos. Therefore, when you introduce the material in this chapter to your students you may want to review with them the discussion in Chapter 1, or use it as a reference point for beginning a discussion of the themes in the current chapter. Explain that the three kinds of appeals are not the only strategies that writers employ when they construct a given argument, nor are they the only strategies that readers look for when analyzing a given argument; rather, emphasize their importance as critical devices.

In addition to the terms *ethos*, *pathos*, and *logos* (which fall under the category of *invention*), this chapter introduces *arrangement* and *style* and explains the rhetorical importance of these activities in presenting arguments.

When you discuss this chapter in your class, you'll probably find it easier to explain the concepts by illustrating them using a particular text as Faigley and Selzer do with the Silko essay from Chapter 11. To reinforce these concepts, you might want to perform a similar analysis on one of your own course readings or on a short reading such as a newspaper editorial or magazine article. (Keep in mind that the analytical techniques introduced in *Good Reasons with Contemporary Arguments* are designed to be used on texts that make a specific argument, so for this exercise you will want to choose an argumentative text. For this reason, avoid choosing articles that are designed to present facts "objectively," such as newspaper reports, for they will make for more difficult classroom discussion.) The discussion questions outlined below are presented generically so they can be applied to either the Silko text or a text of your own choosing.

Explain at the outset that a "rhetorical analysis" is a term that refers to analyzing arguments. Also, you may want to return to the classes' earlier discussion of "rhetoric," since it is a term much abused. Pundits and politicians use the term to refer to hollow or empty speech. An Austin newspaper once ran the headline: "Texas Voters Want Facts, Not Rhetoric." Prominent political figures have accused their opponents of "mouthing mere rhetoric," or making statements that go nowhere. We encourage you to steer the students toward a fairer and more historically informed understanding of the term. As Faigley and Selzer note in *Good Reasons with Contemporary Arguments*, Aristotle defined rhetoric as the art of finding the best available means of persuasion in any situation. The term also historically refers to a staple of the traditional university education. English literature departments as we know them today are a fairly recent invention, and while they teach strong reading and writing skills, their main focus is the subject of so-called literary texts. Emphasize to your students that rhetoric courses teach students how to articulate and effectively communicate material that is not discipline specific. Encourage them to apply the skills they will be learning to the work they do in their other classes, and to their work and other social activities "off campus."

Invention

When teaching ethos, pathos, and logos, as well as the other new terms introduced in this chapter, be sure to emphasize that they do not have the same meanings as their English counterparts but rather are specific terminology with new meanings that the students will need to memorize and become comfortable with. Ethos means something more specific than "ethical," a "pathetic" appeal has very little to do with the ordinary definition of "pathetic," and discussions of a text's "logical" appeal can concern much more than its author's use of reason.

Ethos Ask your students to consider the trustworthiness of the writer based on the information in the text itself and not on any secondary source information or any prior knowledge about the author of the text. Are there any inconsistencies or seeming contradictions in the given text that lead the students to doubt the trustworthiness of the author?

Pathos Explain to your students that writers use pathetic appeals in order to create a kind of pact between themselves and their readers. Such appeals cultivate common ground between writer and reader. Pathetic appeals work by provoking a particular emotional response in the audience. For example, if a writer is claiming that a particular law is unfair, he or she will make remarks that provoke the reader's anger about the given law. If the writer is claiming that a particular community is being abused, he or she will make remarks that provoke the reader's sympathy for the given community. Ask your students to identify the most salient emotional appeal in the given text. Then, ask them what particular values underlie the emotional appeal.

Logos Here, you will want to emphasize again that logical appeals refer to strong connections in a given argument. In particular, we can see these kinds of appeals being made when the author refers to or enlists a hard fact or other material piece of evidence. Ask your students to differentiate between evidence that is accepted as factual or rarely disputed (for example a law or other piece of legislation, a physical event, a statistical finding) and evidence that is disputed. Also, emphasize that writers selectively choose hard facts, so just because the hard fact itself is indisputable does not mean the given argument (the argument that enlists that hard fact) cannot be disputed.

Finally, don't worry if your students (or you yourself) are having trouble distinguishing between these three appeals. They are inseparable. Thus, when you explain the appeals to your students, emphasize that when they write a rhetorical analysis they will probably find that in many instances a given feature of the text can be talked about as an ethical appeal, or a pathetic appeal, or a logical appeal.

Arrangement and Style

Ask your students to review Faigley and Selzer's analysis of Leslie Marmon Silko's essay "The Border Patrol State" (in Chapter 11), particularly their discussion of Silko's *arrangement* and *style.* Then, ask your students to read another essay (perhaps the student essay by T. Jonathan Jackson included in this chapter) and comment on the author's arrangement and style. Ask them in what ways is this arrangement different from Silko's arrangement? In what ways is this style different from Silko's style?

Contextual Analysis

As *Good Reasons with Contemporary Arguments* explains, a rhetorical *textual* analysis typically uses "rhetorical concepts to analyze the feature of texts." In contrast, a rhetorical *contextual* analysis focuses on the larger conversations going on around and about texts. Such analysis does not see the text as self-contained but as part of a larger historic or cultural conversation. If, when you discuss rhetorical textual analysis with your students, you use the Jordan and Silko essays to illustrate your remarks, perhaps you can choose a different text to work with when you discuss contextual analysis. For example, use a short poem, an advertisement, or a newspaper editorial (again, this discussion will proceed more smoothly if you choose a text that makes an explicit argument). Emphasize to your students that for a rhetorical *contextual* analysis they need to "step outside" of the given text in order to be able to "step into it." Working with a given text, ask the students about the biographical facts of the author and his or her other work; about the context of publication of the given text; and, about the kinds of larger political or social conversations that the text seems to be participating in or contributing to. If you teach in a classroom that offers students access to the Internet, you might elect some individual students or groups of students to begin to research these

27

questions online and present their findings to the rest of the class, providing you with an opportunity to discuss not only the context of the text in question, but also the use (and misuse) of Internet sources.

JORDAN, "STATEMENT ON THE ARTICLES OF IMPEACHMENT"

4. What is Jordan's central argument? What is her purpose in making this argument?
5. What textual features does Jordan use to establish her ethos, appeal to her audience's emotions, or make her arguments? (For example, look at her use of quotations from the U.S. Constitution, James Madison, and other sources on the nature of impeachment.)
6. How does the context that Jordan establishes at the beginning of her speech—specifically her references to her African American heritage and use of the word "inquisitor"—affect its overall impact? What changes would the deletion of these contextual features make on the impact of the speech?
7. If you have already had your students read Chapters 8 or 15, on definitional arguments and oral presentations, ask them how Jordan's use of the techniques of definitional argument or oral presentations can be used to analyze this text.

Sample Student Rhetorical Analysis: JACKSON, "AN ARGUMENT OF REASON AND PASSION: BARBARA JORDAN'S 'STATEMENT ON THE ARTICLES OF IMPEACHMENT' "

1. What is Jackson's argument? What is his purpose in making this argument?
2. Ask your students, either individually or in small groups, to label each analytical paragraph in Jackson's essay as being either textual or contextual. It is likely that your students will find it difficult to pick just one label for some paragraphs, or that some have identified a paragraph as being a textual analysis while others have labeled the same paragraph as being a contextual analysis. As a group, discuss the reasons for these different interpretations in relation to Faigley and Selzer's claim that most analyses are combinations of the two approaches.

3. As a group, reread Jackson's analysis of Jordan's use of sources (in the essay's third paragraph). Ask your students if they find Jackson's argument about these "reputable sources" to be sufficient or convincing. Could the same type of argument be made in this context about Internet sources? About the French Constitution? Why or why not? How does the context in which these sources were created, and the context of Jordan's use of them as a member of the House of Representatives, affect the authority of those sources? How does it affect Jordan's authority?

4. Ask your students if they find Jackson's conclusion (on page 3 of his essay) convincing. Why or why not? How did Jackson's ethos or his pathetic and logical appeals affect their reactions?

IN-CLASS ACTIVITIES

• A challenge in teaching ethos is to give students a sense of the many ways in which ethos is (or is not) effectively established. Choose the rhetorical situation of writing a term paper or writing an editorial in the college newspaper. Then, ask your students to make a list of all that a writer in one (or both) of these situations must do to appear credible. What could a writer do to damage his or her credibility? Hopefully, the students will recognize that nearly every component of an argument can be construed as an issue of ethos: from a writer's willingness to consider possible rebuttals to his or her argument, to the sources he or she uses, to the grammar and formatting of his or her paragraphs. Hopefully, too, the students will recognize that determining a writer's ethos, or "credibility," does not boil down to a fixed set of questions to ask. In short, when considering ethos, everything matters, and authors must make their decisions on a case-by-case basis.

SHORT ASSIGNMENTS

• Choose a one-page advertisement from a newspaper or magazine. Have students write a short paper, about 200 words in length, in which they identify one pathetic, one ethical, and one logical appeal. Then, have the students swap their papers with another student to see if what they have identified as a pathetic or ethical or logical appeal has been so identified by their peer, and what other content in the text their peer has identified in the advertisement as a pathetic, ethical, or logical appeal. Ask them how the context in which the advertisement appeared—the audience of the magazine or newspaper, the story or stories that surrounded it—affected their analysis.

• Choose a short story or non-fictional narrative. Divide your students into groups of two, and have each pair write two short papers, each about 200 words in length. One paper will be a rhetorical textual analysis of the text. The student who prepares this paper will comment on how persuasive the narrative is, based on the *arrangement* and *style* that the author uses. The other paper will be a rhetorical contextual analysis. The student who writes this paper will comment on how persuasive the narrative is, based on the biographical facts about the writer and the larger political conversation that informs the given narrative. Ask 1–2 pairs of students to present their findings to the class. Hopefully, students will see that interpretations of texts depend to a large extent on the particular critical tools that they bring to the given text.

Chapter 6: Analyzing Visual Arguments

Arguments that students come across in the course of their academic study and arguments that students are confronted with outside of the class environment are not confined to verbal texts. Thus, this chapter discusses visual texts like graphics, photographs, and charts and graphs. It discusses this visual material either as texts that can stand by themselves or as texts that are used as *evidence* in support of a larger (verbal) argument.

At the beginning of this chapter, Faigley and Selzer return to the definition of an argument in Chapter 1 as a claim with reasons, asking if images, which often lack reasons, can be considered arguments. You may want to review this section of Chapter 1 when discussing this chapter with your students.

If you are planning to allow your students to use visuals in their own papers, or if you are going to have them submit visual assignments, emphasize that the methods for *analyzing* visual arguments outlined in this chapter can also be used as guidelines for *making* visual arguments.

Finally, you may want to discuss how the visual aspects of the layout of a purely textual argument can affect its reception. You may provide examples from newspapers, magazines, and scholarly and popular books and show how the visual layout of each medium affects the reader's perception of the text.

Sample Student Visual Analysis: YAMASHITA, "GOT RODDICK?"

1. What is Yamashita's central argument? What is the purpose of this argument? What reasons are used to support this argument?
2. What main visual evidence does Yamashita rely upon in order to make her argument? How does she connect this visual evidence to her written argument?

3. How does Yamashita's use of visuals in this text affect her ethos? Could she have made the same argument without visuals? Why or why not?

IN-CLASS ACTIVITIES

• Have your students choose a photograph from a recent magazine or newspaper article. Ask the students to interpret the photo (identify its argument) before they read the accompanying article or caption. Then, have them repeat their analysis after reading the accompanying text(s). Choose a few students to share their results with the class.

• Have your students read Edward Tufte's analysis of the Boeing PowerPoint slides addressing the damage to the space shuttle Columbia in his essay "PowerPoint Does Rocket Science—and Better Techniques for Technical Reports" (you can find the complete text at Tufte's Web site, www.edwardtufte.com, by searching for the title). As a class, discuss the visual features of the text—for example, font size of different sections of text or the emphasis of outline levels—and Tufte's analysis of the impact of these slides. As a follow-up exercise, have your students find examples of texts that are similarly visually confusing and bring them to class to share with each other.

• Ask your students to bring to class an essay that they wrote either for this class or for another one. Discuss with your class the visual or typographic features of several of the essays, including the font style, the spacing, and the margins. Ask them to consider what they would do to improve these visual features of the paper.

• Bring to class a selection of full-page advertisements found in a magazine. Ask your students to consider which of the advertisements is the most visually effective and why. Ask your students what features of a less visually effective advertisement could be changed in order to make the advertisement more effective. In this exercise, ask the students if any one of the visual items or features in the advertisement is unnecessary, inappropriate, or unclear. Also, you may want to use this activity to remind the students to think about how the *form* that an argument takes will affect the *content* or message of the argument as well as the reception of that message by an audience.

SHORT ASSIGNMENTS

• Have the students write short responses to the questions under the section "Evaluating Charts and Graphs."

• Have the students bring to class a photograph from a newspaper or periodical of an event or of a person.. Ask them to write a short *textual* visual analysis of the photograph. They will need to comment on the ethical, pathetic, and logical appeals of the visual content of the photograph.

• If your classroom has the appropriate technology, select a random personal page from MySpace (myspace.com), and have your students write a short *textual* analysis of that page, focusing on its visual elements. Discuss the possibility of conducting a *contextual* analysis of the page when they do not know the person who posted it.

• Have the students bring to class a personal photograph of an event or of a person whom they know. Ask them to write a short *contextual* visual analysis of the photograph. They will need to discuss the identity of the photographer and the circumstances surrounding the taking of the photograph. As with the above-suggested assignment, this exercise can help students understand that texts can produce very different meanings or make very different arguments depending on the critical tools that a reader employs to "read" these texts.

Part 3: Writing Arguments

Chapter 7: Putting Good Reasons into Action

Explain to your students that while the material that they will be learning about in Part 3 of *Good Reasons with Contemporary Arguments* distinguishes between certain types of argument, the students probably have come across many arguments in "real life" that are composed of combinations of types of these arguments. Illustrate your explanation with a newspaper article. Ask the students to identify language or strategies employed by the author that evidence one or more of the following: definitional language, causal language, evaluative language, a narrative, a rebuttal language, or a proposal. Make clear the central point that people generally use argumentative strategies in combinations to propose some form of action.

That said, also make clear that while the students will be employing many of the aforesaid strategies in a single paper assignment, if the assignment asks them to perform a definition argument, they should focus mainly on language and strategies that show their reader that they are making a definition argument; if the assignment asks them to perform a causal argument, they should focus mainly on language and strategies that show their reader that they are making a causal argument.

IN-CLASS ACTIVITIES

• *Finding Good Reasons: What Do We Mean by Diversity?* After drafting their proposals, create a forum—perhaps online on your course Web site, or at a free blogging service like WordPress or Blogger—for your students to post and respond to each other's proposals. Require your students to post comments on each other's proposals, responding to their classmates' ideas.

• It is difficult when teaching a writing course to dissolve the walls of the classroom entirely. That is to say, it is difficult to design assignments that don't seem like assignments. There is no getting around the fact that, in the end, you're an instructor and you read and assess your students' work. However, it is possible to design assignments that require students to get involved in some issue of local or national concern. You might begin this process by bringing to class a newspaper that contains a number of letters to the editor concerning a particular local issue. Have students draft a brief letter in response to one or several of the published letters. Then, have students trade their letters and discuss what they wrote and why they wrote it in the way they did. The point is to get students to make a connection between what they learn in your class and the world outside.

SHORT ASSIGNMENTS

• Have students (individually or in groups) read a newspaper article that covers a particular event. Ask the students to answer briefly one or more of the following questions:

- Identify a critical term or concept in the argument: How is the author *defining* or using this term or concept in his or her argument? What other meanings could the term or concept have outside of this rhetorical situation?

- Is the particular event the result (effect) of certain *causes*? Does the author explicitly or implicitly identify these causes? What are some possible causes for the event that the author does not address?

- Is the author negatively or positively criticizing the event? Is the author's main purpose to *evaluate* the event or is there some other main purpose?

- Does the author take into account counter arguments and persuasively *rebut* them?

- If the author is addressing a particular problem, does he or she *propose* any solutions to the problem? If not what are some possible solutions?

Chapter 8: Definition Arguments

Most controversial debates can be understood as questions of definition. Is wearing animal fur unethical? Is keeping animals in zoos cruelty to animals? Is euthanasia murder? Is cheerleading a sport? Definitions matter even in debates that don't seem to hinge on definitional issues. For instance, proposals for protecting children from pornographic material on the World Wide Web require people to consider exactly what pornography is.

When teaching students about definition arguments, the following formula can be used as an example of the components necessary for making this kind of claim:

> **X** (individual feature or component) belongs to the general class or category **Y** because it (**X**) possesses certain criteria **A, B, C** that make up the general class or category **Y**.

The Y term can be thought of as a contested category—that is, as a category that needs to be defined in a particular rhetorical situation: a just law, murder, a lie, a sport, and so on. In an arguable claim, the X term can be thought of as something that might or might not fall into that Y category (other textbooks have referred to X as a "borderline case"). The criteria A, B, C are the characteristics that define that Y category. These criteria describe the qualities that make Y distinct. To be considered an example of Y, X must meet all of these criteria.

To demonstrate to your students how categories need to be defined in a particular rhetorical situation, ask them, for example, whether or not they think the *Birth of Venus* (individual **X**), by the neoclassical French painter Alexandre Cabanel, which depicts a woman clad in a thin garment and in a position that suggests she is having some kind of ecstatic experience, is pornography (general class **Y**).

As Faigley and Selzer note in *Good Reasons with Contemporary Arguments*, an extended definition argument requires that you set out the criteria that define the Y category, argue for them as the rhetorical situation

36

requires, and then show that X meets all of those criteria. This can be exceptionally difficult to do. Not only do you have to offer criteria that your audience will accept; you also have to show that X meets those criteria. In a sense, an extended definition argument is two separate arguments: one establishing the criteria, the other matching X to the criteria. And as your students will find, establishing satisfactory criteria is no easy task. In this situation, it is helpful to remind your students that these criteria depend on their audience's concerns, so a crucial step in determining the criteria is clearly establishing who that audience will be.

Finally, we should note that the formula above—though it can help students become more comfortable with the nature and requirements of definition arguments—shouldn't obscure the fact that definition arguments do not exist in isolation. Require students to recognize what is at stake in definitional arguments, particularly in the ones they write. Scott McCloud, for instance, takes some care to define comics because he hopes to show both that the current definitions of the term are narrow and based on stereotypes, and that the "potential for comics is limitless and exciting." In Martin Luther King Jr.'s definition of unjust laws (with regard to his appeal to people to disobey segregation ordinances), he makes it clear that writers need to take into account their particular audience. In the case of King's argument, he first sought to impress upon his primary audience of eight white clergymen that segregation laws (X) belonged to the larger category of unjust laws (Y) according to two criteria that this particular audience would appreciate. He then sought to convince a larger secular audience that segregation laws fell into the category of unjust laws by adding two more criteria that would appeal to this audience's values.

A crucial point you will want to make to your students is that when it is time for them to make their own definition argument, they will need to clearly demonstrate what the benefits of accepting that definition will be. That is, they must make clear the *exigence* of their definitions. Their concerns will often go beyond mere semantics, or what individual words mean. Rather, when they make their definitional arguments, they should do so with the purpose of effecting a change in the world around them.

McCLOUD, "SETTING THE RECORD STRAIGHT"

1. What is McCloud's central claim? What is the purpose of McCloud's argument? What reasons and evidence support it?
2. Identify the criteria that make up McCloud's formal definition of a comic. Have your students fill out the definition argument formula substituting the details of McCloud's argument for X, Y, and A, B, C. Are there any parts of the argument that are made by the images in the comic that are difficult to adequately translate into text? What are some other ways that McCloud benefits from making his argument both visually and textually?
3. Are there any visual texts that do not fit the formal definition of a comic but that operate as comics? Alternatively, are there any visual texts that fit the formal definition of comics but do not operate as such?

Sample Student Definition Argument: NGUYEN, "SPEECH DOESN'T HAVE TO BE PRETTY TO BE PROTECTED"

1. What is Nguyen's central claim? What is the purpose of Nguyen's argument? What reasons support it?
2. Have your students rephrase Nguyen's argument in the form of the definition formula described in this chapter. Are any of the sections missing from Nguyen's argument? How does the arrangement of Nguyen's essay differ from the arrangement of the definition formula?
3. Ask your students how the implications of Nguyen's argument go beyond merely defining what terms like "free speech" mean. Can they think of examples from their school or communities where the definition of terms like "trespassing," "public," or "private" have a similarly broad impact?
4. What is the importance of Nguyen's research to the argument he makes? Do your students find his sources credible? Why or why not? Would his argument be as convincing without this source material to draw from?

IN-CLASS ACTIVITIES

• *Finding Good Reasons: What is Parody?* Find a satirical text—perhaps an episode of *South Park* or *The Colbert Report*—and discuss with your students the impact of that parody. What claims are being made by the parody? Who or what is the target of its humor?

• With your students, develop a long list of X terms (e.g., cheerleading, a political demonstration, a union strike, purchasing clothes from a company that uses cheap "offshore" labor) and Y terms (e.g., a sport, public disturbance, patriotism). Write each term on a slip of paper and have students blindly choose one from each list. Then, ask students to argue that the X term that they've chosen fits into the category represented by the Y term they've chosen. Students will have to argue for absurd, randomly generated claims such as "cheerleading is a public disturbance" and "purchasing clothes from a company that uses offshore labor is an act of patriotism." Whether or not the activity generates serious responses or laughter, it will give students practice in thinking about what's required in making an extended definitional argument. To raise the stakes (and the level of absurdity), you might also have students draw another slip of paper, this one describing a particular rhetorical context. So, for example, some student might be asked to argue that cheerleading is a form of public disturbance in a Sunday church service.

• For those of you who are a little more wary of making fun of serious issues, perhaps you may want to approach the aforesaid X and Y terms in a less frivolous manner. For example, ask the students if they think that cheerleading (X) should be recognized as a sport (the larger category Y). What would be the purpose of demonstrating that the X term belongs to the definition or category Y?

SHORT ASSIGNMENTS

• Challenge your students to find the definitional claims at work in local, state, or federal debates that concern them. Ask them to write 1–2 paragraphs in response to one or more of the following sets of questions:

- What definitional issues are at stake in the debate over U.S. military involvement in Iraq?

- Should an SUV be considered a truck or a car, and what is at stake in the definition?

- What is a "health bar" as opposed to a "candy bar," and why would a company that makes so-called health bars want to be able to legally advertise its products as "health bars"?

- What is the *formal* (dictionary) definition of fast food, what are some *examples* of fast foods, and what kinds of foods do not fit the *formal* definition of fast food but *operate* as fast food?

- What is the *formal* definition of pornography, and in what kinds of rhetorical situations does a sexually explicit verbal or visual text *operate* or *not operate* as pornography?

- What is the formal definition of cruelty to animals according to PETA (People for the Ethical Treatment of Animals)? What are some *examples* of animal treatment that PETA considers to be acts of animal cruelty, and would a zoo or a biomedical research laboratory regard such treatment as acts of animal cruelty?

• Ask students to find a newspaper article that doesn't appear to deal with definitions and then to uncover the key definitional terms at work in the argument. In other words, what are the unstated definitions of key terms that the author assumes his or her readers share?

• Have each student in your course prepare a definitional claim of his or her choice in 1–2 paragraphs. This is a more difficult assignment than it seems. Inevitably you will find that a number of students will submit evaluative claims (see Chapter 10) as definitional. For example, some students will want to argue that a celebrity is or is not a good role model. We also recommend that you devise some means of encouraging students to think of *unique* claims. The purpose of the assignment is for students to develop a number of claims that you can afterwards discuss in class, and that students may draw from when writing their own definitional arguments.

Chapter 9: Causal Arguments

The causal argument paper can be one of the most difficult writing assignments for students. Many times students will write an evaluation of a given problem or effect instead of writing the causes that *resulted in* or *led to* the given problem or effect. The skills that they are required to master to construct a strong causal argument, however, are the same skills they will use when they come to writing an evaluation argument. Many students may not have encountered these skills earlier in their academic careers. These skills are: the ability to present the full breadth and complexity of an issue while making an argument, and the ability to qualify a claim so that it neither overreaches nor oversimplifies the problem it addresses. Emphasize that issues worth arguing about are complex and rarely the result of direct causation.

PAUL, "THE REAL MARRIAGE PENALTY"

1. What is Paul's central argument? What is her purpose in making this argument? What reasons does she provide to support it?
2. Which of the kinds of causation—single cause, multiple effect; multiple cause, single effect; chain reaction—described by Faigley and Selzer does Paul use in her essay? Does she use more than one?
3. One of the major difficulties in making any causal argument is distinguishing between causation and correlation, or between an effect that is prompted by an action or event and one that merely occurs after that action or event in time. How does Paul deal with this problem in her essay? Are you and your students convinced that the causes she describes led to the effects she attributes to them? Can you and your students brainstorm other causes that might have led to these particular effects?

41

RAINE, "WHY SHOULD I BE NICE TO YOU? COFFEE SHOPS AND THE POLITICS OF GOOD SERVICE"

1. What is Raine's central argument? What is her purpose in making this argument? What reasons does she supply to support it?
2. Ask your students if Raine's conclusions about service work apply to their own experiences working in the service industry. Why or why not?
3. Which kind of causation—single cause, multiple effect; multiple cause, single effect; chain reaction—described by Faigley and Selzer does Raine make use of in her essay? Does she use more than one?
4. Compare the style of Raine's essay with that of Paul's essay. For example, how do the opening paragraphs of Raine's essay differ from those of Paul's essay? How are the two different with regard to their use of source materials and other evidence? Ask your students why these differences exist. If they can't think of any answers, discuss the different contexts of their publication and their differing subject matter.
5. Raine suggests that one cause of poor customer service in coffee shops and other venues is that customer "throughput" is more highly valued by the corporations that own these businesses than good customer experiences. She concludes her essay by describing how she asserted her humanity as a barista by "be[ing] rude." What are some possible effects of these two causes that are not explored in this essay?

IN-CLASS ACTIVITIES

• *Finding Good Reasons: Why are Americans Gaining Weight?* One of the contributing factors to American obesity mentioned in this box is the dependence of Americans on their cars. Discuss with your students how greater availability (or use) of public transportation might help alleviate this problem. Alternatively, ask if their communities are designed so that they could walk more and drive less. If not, how could their community be redesigned to make this possible?

• In completing a causal argument assignment, students might ask why you insist that they narrow and focus their claims. Explain your insistence in terms of ethos. What, for example, would their response be to someone who makes a causal argument but doesn't "get" the issue they ostensibly aim to address? Illustrate your point by giving them an example of such an argument. Advertisements, letters to the editor, and brief editorials work well for this sort of discussion. Read the piece together as a class and discuss students' initial responses to the argument.

• As we noted earlier in this manual, students need to be instructed to actively use resources such as Mill's four methods of finding causes. Bring to class a list of 2–3 current issues that pose a variety of causal dilemmas. Societal trends tend to be good topics for this sort of discussion (e.g., the decrease in the value of an undergraduate degree, the death of etiquette, the rise in the divorce rate, the prevalence of—and backlash against—popular patriotism). As a class, find several narrow subtopics (e.g., grade inflation, divorce rates in a specific population, debates about terrorism on campus) within each of these broader topics and decide which of Mill's methods would work best for each.

• In small groups, have students make a list of the number of causal claims they've recently heard at work, around town, or on campus. Then, have them examine those claims, and sketch out the argumentative strategy they could use to argue 1–2 of the claims. Encourage students to use Mill's four methods for finding causes.

SHORT ASSIGNMENTS

• Have students find a short causal argument that they can analyze in 1–2 pages of writing. In their analysis, they should address the main claim and the main reasons (causes) the author provides. They should also try to identify the author's methodology. Which one of the four methods did the author use: *the common factor, the single difference, the concomitant variation,* or *the process of elimination* method? Was this method effective? Why or why not? If the method was not successful, students should suggest another possible method of approaching the argument.

• Have the students write a short causal argument—1–2 pages in length—that addresses one of the issues bulleted below. For these assignments, the students will have to do some brief research. However, emphasize to them that the point of the exercise is for them to construct a causal argument as opposed to constructing any other kind of argument. The assignment is meant to give them practice in using causal language and prepare them, therefore, for writing an extensive causal argument. Thus, emphasize to your students that as long as they properly cite secondary source information, they can rely on such information to build their very short causal argument.

- The increase (or decrease) in growth of a given city or given neighborhood

- The increase in consumption of commercially bottled water as opposed to tap water

- The increase in number of students applying to law school

• If you plan to assign a long-paper causal argument, ask your students to save the research they do for their short causal paper assignment. They can use this research to develop a topic of their own choice when they come to write the long-paper causal argument. For the long-paper causal argument, ask your students to focus on a topic that has some bearing on or in some way ties to the topic that they earlier researched.

Chapter 10: Evaluation Arguments

As Faigley and Selzer note in *Good Reasons with Contemporary Arguments*, an evaluation claim takes the following form:

> **X** is a good (bad, the best, the worst) **Y** if measured by criteria **A**, **B**, and **C**.

As this formula makes clear, evaluation arguments are similar to definition arguments in several important ways. In both, the writer must determine and, when necessary, argue for a set of criteria, and then show how someone or something either meets or does not meet those criteria. However, in an evaluation argument there is little question whether X is an example of Y. That is to say, the author and his or her audience are sure that Wendy's is a fast-food restaurant, or that Angelina Jolie is an actress, or that Jay-Z is a rap musician. Your concern is not definition but quality. How good is the fast-food operation of Wendy's? Why is Angelina Jolie popular? What makes a good rapper good?

Have students consider the range of evaluative terms available to them. The formula above uses the terms "good," "bad," "best," and "worst," but the range of evaluative terms is much broader than this and depends on the kind of criteria that we use when we make evaluations: aesthetic, practical, or moral.

Emphasize to your students that when they develop their own evaluation claims they ought to choose the Y term carefully. The Y term should not be too narrow or too broad. In the sample evaluation argument that *Good Reasons with Contemporary Arguments* provides, the Y term refers to sending people into space (as opposed to using human robots). If the Y term had been simply "space travel," it would have been a very broad term. If the Y term had been the Columbia space shuttle flight that resulted in the death of seven astronauts, it would have been a very narrow term.

Also, suggest to your students that when they are deciding what to evaluate, they should test their Y terms by listing five or six examples of X

45

terms that could be considered as members of that category. For example, ask your students to review Faigley and Selzer's short discussion of the college rankings in *U.S. News & World Report*. What other methods could be used to rank colleges and universities? Could (or should) these methods be based on the criteria used to rank businesses, for example? Advise your students that when they write their rough draft of an evaluative argument they may find that they want to revise their evaluative terms and their Y terms. Explain that this is not uncommon at all. Even the most sophisticated writers often end up having to revise their initial claims.

Finally, explain to students that the criteria they develop in an evaluation argument are as important as the criteria they develop in a definition argument. It is easy for students to list criteria based on their individual likes and dislikes. Encourage them to use criteria in ways that make their evaluative argument persuasive for their primary and secondary audiences. For example, a student is writing an evaluation of a particular pizzeria. She argues that it is the "best" pizzeria in town because she is a vegetarian and the pizzeria offers a larger selection of vegetarian pizzas. Emphasize to the student the need to consider people other than herself. In what ways could she make her argument acceptable to readers who are not vegetarians but who, nonetheless, might like a pizzeria that offers a wider selection of vegetarian pizzas?

DYSON, "GANGSTA RAP AND AMERICAN CULTURE"

1. What is Dyson's central argument? What is his purpose in making this argument? What reasons and evidence does he use to support that argument?
2. What type of evaluation is Dyson making? Aesthetic, practical, moral, or some combination of the three?
3. How is the evaluative argument Dyson makes different from a definitional argument? If students have a hard time answering this question, consider having them outline Dyson's argument using the definitional formula discussed in Chapter 8, as well as the evaluative formula discussed in this chapter. If you do so, it is likely that you will have some students who argue that Dyson is, in fact, making a

definition argument. If this is the case, use this ambiguity to underscore the fact that few arguments are purely definitional, evaluative, etc., but rather incorporate elements of many argumentative types.

4. Consider the following quotation from paragraph 10: "Gangsta rap is no less legitimate because many 'gangstas' turn out to be middle-class blacks faking homeboy roots. This fact simply focuses attention on the genre's essential constructedness, its literal artifice. Much of gangsta rap makes voyeuristic whites and naïve blacks think they're getting a slice of authentic ghetto life when in reality they're being served colorful exaggerations." Ask your students if they are convinced by the claims Dyson makes in this section. If they are, how do these claims affect their acceptance/rejection of Dyson's evaluation? If not, ask them to explain why.

Sample Student Evaluation Argument: GIDDENS, "STOP LOSS OR 'LOSS OF TRUST' "

1. What is Giddens's central argument? What is his purpose in making this argument? What reasons and evidence does he use to support that argument?

2. What kind of evaluation is Giddens making of the stop loss program: aesthetic, practical, moral, or some combination of the three?

3. Ask your students if they can determine what audience Giddens's essay is addressed to. Then, ask them how these audience concerns affect their reactions to the essay: Do they agree or disagree with Giddens? How can they use what they have learned from this audience analysis to help improve their own writing?

4. How do the opening paragraphs of the essay, where Giddens explains his own experience with military recruitment and the experience of his cousin, affect his ethos in the essay? Is this effect positive or negative? Be sure to encourage students to provide specific examples from the essay when they answer.

IN-CLASS ACTIVITIES

• *Finding Good Reasons: What is the Best Alternative Fuel?* Have your students brainstorm additional criteria for evaluating an alternative fuel, and then, as a group, have them rank all the criteria from most to least important. Ask them how their experience in making these rankings is similar to the political processes that determine government fuel policies?

• Have students make a list of things—computers, dorm rooms, college courses, running shoes—and then come up with the most compelling evaluative term to apply to each. Have them make a list for each kind of criterion: aesthetic, practical, and moral.

• It is difficult to develop a manageable and meaningful Y term. It's also difficult to anticipate how your audience will interpret your Y term. As a class, develop a list of broad Y terms. Then, break students into groups of 2–3, and have them come up with as many subcategories as they can for one or several of the Y terms. (For "movie," they might list comedy, romantic comedy, drama, epic). Then, select one of these subcategories and have each group list ten or fifteen examples that fit the given category. Compare the groups' responses. Did each come up with the same list? Chances are that they didn't. The chances are also good that many of the items listed will not be easily comparable. You can use this exercise, then, as a way of discussing how evaluative claims must be geared to specific rhetorical situations. For example, in some situations it makes no sense to compare *Manhattan* and *There's Something About Mary* as comedies. In other situations, however, the two movies might be effectively compared. Establishing the appropriateness of the context, then, is essential to an evaluative argument.

SHORT ASSIGNMENTS

• Ask students to find a review of a movie, book, restaurant or musical group with which they strongly disagree. Ask them to write a detailed response to it. Do they disagree with the reviewer's Y term? Is the reviewer using the wrong type of criteria (aesthetic, practical, moral)? Is there a problem with the criteria? The reviewer's ethos?

• Ask students to find another essay in the textbook that combines an evaluative claim with another type of argument. Then have students write a paragraph discussing how the author uses the two types of argument. Students should also evaluate whether or not this combination is effective and why.

Chapter 11: Narrative Arguments

As Faigley and Selzer point out, narrative arguments can succeed sometimes when other forms of argument fail. These arguments persuade by
illustration or by *implicit* argument as opposed to *explicit* argument.
They also often offer a sort of intimacy that more formal and academic
arguments rarely achieve. They are the stuff of both fictional texts and
non-fictional texts. When you introduce this chapter to your students, ask
your students about a novel or short story or film that they have read or
seen that impressed them (if they are reluctant to answer, suggest recent
films like *Children of Men, Knocked Up,* or *I Am Legend* or television
shows like *The Sopranos*). Review Dagoberto Gilb's narrative essay "My
Landlady's Yard" with your students, and ask them what makes this narrative so compelling. Emphasize to your class that the narratives made up
by novelists, short story writers, film artists, and other writers contain,
and make, powerful arguments. Such arguments might not have the same
impact or might not address the same audience if produced in a different
form such as in the form of a journal article or newspaper commentary.

Emphasize to your students that narrative arguments are very useful devices that writers use *within* other kinds of arguments. If you have time,
review with your students the discussion in Chapter 1 of Rachel Carson's
Silent Spring. As *Good Reasons* makes clear, Carson's use of a narrative
was instrumental in the book's success. She uses a narrative within an
argument that informed people about DDT and that sought to restrict future use of DDT.

If you don't plan to assign your students a major narrative argument assignment, encourage them to use narratives in the other arguments that
they will be making throughout the term. For example, your students can
introduce their causal arguments with a narrative or anecdote, or they can
incorporate within their evaluation argument a short narrative or personal
story. Whatever the students choose, emphasize to them that they should
follow the pointers offered in this chapter. First, the person who makes a
narrative argument needs to be credible. Second, the incident (or experi-

ence) described needs to be representative somehow of the experience of the audience. As we note in the text, we don't ban bananas simply because one person slipped on a banana peel.

SILKO, "THE BORDER PATROL STATE"

1. What is the argument of Silko's narrative? What is her purpose in making this argument?
2. What reasons does Silko use to support her claims? Which of her reasons are explicit; which are implicit?
3. How does Silko's ethos or credibility affect her use of narrative to support her claims?
4. What risks does Silko take in using these narratives? What benefits does using narratives give her?

GILB, "MY LANDLADY'S YARD"

1. What is the argument of Gilb's narrative? What is his purpose in making this argument? What reasons does he use to support it?
2. How does this story affect the emotions of the audience (pathos)? How does this effect impact the effectiveness of Gilb's argument
3. Is Gilb's narrative true? Is it applicable to a wider audience? These are tricky questions to consider when discussing a personal story. Ask your students what the implications might be of answering "no" to either of these questions. (You might also find it helpful to introduce and discuss recent scandals over the truthfulness of claims made by memoir authors.)

IN-CLASS ACTIVITIES

• This subject matter of this chapter offers an opportunity for you to discuss fictional works with your students, giving them examples of different kinds of narrative arguments that they can model. For example, photocopy for your students a short story by Hemingway ("The Short Happy Life of Francis Macomber," "The Hills Like White Elephants"), Richard Wright (any one of the stories in the collection Uncle Tom's Children), Charlotte Perkins Gilman ("The Yellow Wallpaper"), Jorge Luis Borges

("The Garden of Forking Paths," "The Aleph") or Cory Doctorow ("Scroogled," "0wnz0red").

Once you have chosen a story, have your students read it for homework, note the date of publication, and briefly research the author and the work in a literary encyclopedia or by an Internet search. Discuss with your students how the author addresses social or political issues by way of a literary narrative. What are some arguments embedded in the narrative? Why did the writer present his or her argument in the form of a literary work and not in the form of a more explicit social or political commentary?

• Bring to class examples of other narrative arguments that are not explicit, such as personal essays, songs, political satires, or cartoons. Discuss the reasons why the author or artist chose to make an implicit rather than an explicit argument, and why he or she chose this particular medium to present the argument. How effective was this choice?

• Ask your students to bring to class two short examples of arguments that use narrative as a rhetorical strategy, choosing one example that is effective and one that is not. Tell them that they can choose their two texts from a variety of different forms: political advertisements, musical recordings, Web sites, editorials, letters to the editor of a newspaper, or transcripts of a speech. Ask the students to comment on what makes one narrative effective and the other one not. Their discussion should address the authors' credibility and whether or not the narratives used appear representative (rather than aberrant or otherwise unique).

SHORT ASSIGNMENTS

• *Finding Good Reasons: Can a Story Make an Argument?* Continue this discussion of narrative arguments by having students search for additional examples of Katrina narratives. Then, have them write a 1–2 page paper evaluating the narratives they found: Are they convincing? Why? How do the criteria of truthfulness and applicability affect their responses to these narratives? What about the rhetorical appeals of ethos, pathos, and logos? What is the importance of these narratives in relation to other kinds of reporting about this event?

52

• Ask students to find a recent newspaper or other journal article that uses a narrative in conjunction with another form of argument. Then, ask them to prepare a short, 1–2-page paper analyzing the effectiveness of this narrative. If it was effective, in what ways could it be made better? If it was not effective, what were the reasons for its failure? Was the narrative too long? Would it be more effective if it were placed elsewhere in the text? Did it adequately illustrate the given argument, or did it veer off on another argument? Was it necessary to illustrate the given argument?

• Have students find an example of a narrative argument that uses humor ineffectively. They should then write a paragraph explaining why humor does not work in this particular argument. Is it because of the situation or topic being addressed? Is it because the author's credibility is questionable? Is it because the humor isn't representative or appropriate for the audience?

Chapter 12: Rebuttal Arguments

Students will use rebuttal arguments frequently in their college careers. Indeed, many writers use the rebuttal as a way to develop or strengthen their own argument. As Faigley and Selzer suggest, when writing a rebuttal, students have available to them two primary strategies: first, they can *refute* the argument they wish to undermine by identifying its shortcomings; second, they can emphasize the positive strengths of the position they wish to support. Additionally, these two strategies can be used independently or in a single rebuttal argument.

When writers *refute* arguments, they might challenge the criteria used in a definitional or evaluative argument, or the description of the problem in a proposal argument, or some of the unexamined assumptions that underpin a narrative argument. They also might challenge the evidence supporting the reasons. They might argue that the evidence is inconclusive, incomplete, or unrepresentative. Or they might provide evidence that suggests an entirely different set of conclusions. It is helpful to describe these different means of refutation for your students, in order to give them models for writing their own rebuttals.

When writers *counter-argue*, they focus more on their own argument than on the shortcomings of their opponent's argument. Review with your students Wilfred Owen's poem "Dulce Et Decorum Est." Ask them to identify the argument of the poem, and point out to them that here Owen does not refute the arguments made *for war*. Rather, he tries to make as strong as possible an argument *against war*.

Remind students that rebuttals should not be thought of in isolation, or as being completely separate from other kinds of argument. In fact, it is likely that they will use the techniques of rebuttal in several papers they write for your class. When writing proposals, for instance, they will examine other possible solutions to the problem that their proposal intends to address. In doing so, it's likely that they will write a 1–2 paragraph rebuttal argument, showing the ways in which the alternative proposal does not address the problem, is based on mistaken assumptions, or is not as practical or effective as its proponents believe.

STEIN, "CROSSING THE LINE"

1. What is the argument of Stein's editorial? What is his purpose in making this argument? What reasons does he give to support it?
2. How important are the rhetorical appeals (ethos, pathos, logos) in determining the effectiveness of Stein's rebuttal?
3. What group(s) are the intended audience for Stein's editorial?
4. How would you characterize the style and tone of this editorial? Compare your initial impression to that of Gregory Rodriguez in his rebuttal essay.

RODRIGUEZ, "ILLEGAL IMMIGRANTS—THEY'RE MONEY"

1. What is the main claim of Rodriguez's rebuttal? What is his purpose in making this argument? What reasons does he give to support it?
2. What argument or arguments is Rodriguez replying to in Stein's editorial? Does he attempt to refute those arguments or provide counter-arguments (or both)?
3. Ask your students if they feel that Rodriguez fairly characterizes Stein's arguments or not. In responding to this question, require them to provide specific examples from each text. How do the results of this investigation change their opinion of Rodriguez's argument? Stein's argument?
4. How would you describe Rodriguez's ethos in this essay? How does it compare to Stein's? What particular reasons influence your answers to these questions? How do your answers to these questions affect your reaction to the two essays?

IN-CLASS ACTIVITIES

Writing instructors do not commonly require their students to write a rebuttal argument as a major assignment. Rather, they ask students to incorporate rebuttal arguments into their definitional, evaluative, causal, or proposal arguments. Therefore, take advantage of in-class activities and short assignments when you introduce rebuttal arguments to your students. For example:

• Review the "fallacies in argument" listed in Chapter 3. Ask the students to bring to class 1–2 "letters to the editor" of a local newspaper. Have the students locate as many fallacies as they can in the arguments made by the authors of the letters. Emphasize to the students that they are *refuting* the given arguments. This will give them a sense of accomplishment and professionalism as writers and readers.

• Ask the students to work as a group on a counterargument that supports the interests of a minority group of people in the community—interests that have not yet been realized or receive little attention by the majority of people in the community. Have the students develop reasons in support of their counterargument. Emphasize to them, however, that their counterargument must be an argument that works toward promoting accord between the minority and majority groups. It ought not be a recipe for further division between the two groups.

• *Finding Good Reasons: Can the Web Be Trusted for Research?* Have your students brainstorm other kinds of Web-based information sources that have offline counterparts (for example, news reporting on blogs vs. news reporting in newspapers, or podcasts vs. radio programs) and apply Faigley and Selzer's analysis of Wikipedia's usefulness and reliability to these sources.

SHORT ASSIGNMENTS

• Have students find another reading in the textbook in which rebuttal is used in combination with another form of argument. Then, have them write a short analysis of this rebuttal, addressing whether or not the author deals fairly with the argument or arguments he or she is responding to and whether or not the author presents himself or herself as credible. The students should also evaluate whether or not the rebuttal is effective in this particular argument and why.

Chapter 13: Proposal Arguments

The formula for a proposal argument is deceptively simple:

We should or should not do X for reasons A, B, C, . . .

What this formula does not capture is the difficulty of making effective proposals. The problems worth writing about are always complicated. As you begin work on a proposal, you see that people have different understandings of what the problem is and how it should be addressed. You see that resources are limited and money is tight. And always there are the questions that all proposals must address: Why do we need to change things in the first place? Are things really so bad?

Proposals often work well as a final assignment. They require students to complete effective research; to address their audience with a clear knowledge of that audience's needs and assumptions; to consider their own ethos; and, finally, to effectively employ the range of arguments presented in this section of *Good Reasons*. We encourage you to have students write proposals that address issues in their own communities.

Students generally want to address issues that cannot be effectively handled in a 5–6 page paper. Even those students who take on narrow topics will find their work more complicated than they first imagined. To emphasize this point, as you get closer to the due date of the proposal assignment, you may want to review with your students the parking example that opens this chapter. Ask them about the process the hypothetical student went through to find an effective proposal that would be convincing to the intended audience—the university president. Encourage students to modify their own proposals in response. Perhaps they should qualify their claims. Perhaps they should challenge the assumptions that have led to a certain state of affairs. Or perhaps they may need to do more research. The challenge that you face as a teacher is considerable: you want to let them narrow their claims themselves, but you also want to guide them so that they can complete the project within the time allotted.

Finally, many instructors assign a proposal argument in the form of a project that the students work on collectively. For example, you can divide your class into groups of 4–6, depending on the size of your class. Direct each group to choose an issue, develop a proposal, and then divide the work of crafting that proposal among the members of the group. Some students should research, some collaborate to write the introduction, some handle possible rebuttals, some conduct the necessary interviews and teacher conferences, and then report back to their peers. The exercise can be difficult to coordinate, of course, and it tends to require a good deal of in-class time. However, as a capstone to a semester's work, it can be quite effective because it requires students to employ many of the skills and concepts they've learned during the term.

HOMER-DIXON AND FRIEDMAN, "COAL IN A NICE SHADE OF GREEN"

1. What is the proposal made in this essay? What is the authors' purpose in making this proposal? What reasons do they give to support it?

2. Have your students review the alternatives to fossil fuel that the authors mention and then dismiss in paragraphs 1–7. What are the grounds for dismissing these alternatives? Are these grounds reasonable; that is, are they appropriate to the problem at hand?

3. Ask your students to reread the brief biographical introductions to Homer-Dixon and Friedman. (If you have time, and the available resources to do so, you may have them supplement this information with information from the Internet.) How does this information affect the authors' collective ethos? (If the students generally agree on one position—their connection to gasification projects harms their ethos—try to complicate that agreement—their connection to these projects makes them trustworthy experts.)

Sample Student Proposal Argument: LEE, "LET'S MAKE IT A REAL MELTING POT WITH PRESIDENTIAL HOPES FOR ALL"

1. What is Lee's proposal? What is the purpose of this proposal? What reasons and evidence support it?
2. Once your students have identified the proposal in Lee's essay, discuss with them the arrangement of this proposal in the body of the essay. What does Lee gain (or lose) by leaving the explicit statement of this proposal until the third page of the essay?
3. How does the inclusion of the Schwarzenegger example on page 2 supplement the example of the adopted child that opens the paper? Does it strengthen the argument made by that narrative, or undermine it? Are the two situations comparable?

IN-CLASS ACTIVITIES

• *Finding Good Reasons: Who Should Make Decisions about Economic Development?* Have your students do a role-playing exercise where they take on the various personas outlined in this info box. Either divide them into three groups or choose three representatives to argue the positions of Wal-Mart, Responsible Growth for Norcross, and the Austin City Council, then have them defend the positions of these groups in the class discussion.

• Have your students review the list of issues provided in *Good Reasons with Contemporary Arguments*, Chapter 3, under the heading "List and Analyze Issues." Have them choose 2–3 issues from this list that address a particular social or political problem. Ask the students to propose some practical solutions to that problem.

• As a class, generate a list of problems around your campus. Decide on one problem to pursue further. Break the students into small groups and have the groups generate possible solutions to the problem. Discuss the proposed solutions as a class, addressing questions of feasibility. Is there clearly a best solution? Discuss how students might develop a proposal for this solution. Is more than one solution possible? Discuss ways in which students might narrow the solutions down to the best, or how they might address multiple solutions in a proposal argument.

SHORT ASSIGNMENTS

• In this chapter, Faigley and Selzer discuss the Education Amendments Act, including Title IX, which prohibits sex discrimination at colleges that receive federal aid. Have students reread this discussion, including the discussion of the three options that were proposed by the Office of Civil Rights (OCR) in order for schools to comply with Title IX. Then ask them to think about other spheres of activity in which women do not have equal representation. Ask your students to write a short paper that offers 1–2 proposals to the problem of unequal representation. Does the proposal call for a specific action to take place? Does it call for a certain action to cease? Does it call for a change in policy? Does it call attention to a particular social issue or ask for a certain point of view to be considered? Or, does it call for something else?

• Have students find 1–2 examples of implicit proposal arguments (advertisements are particularly good sources of these implicit proposals). Ask them to write a short explication of the argument's claims, its structure, and its appeals. Is this argument best made to its particular audience in this fashion or would it benefit from being more explicit? Why or why not?

• Proposal arguments often incorporate several different types of argument (definition or narrative, for example). Have students look over the other readings in the book to find other proposal arguments. Then, have the students list the other types of arguments they find in these proposals and explain the purpose each type serves within the context of the proposal argument.

Part 4: Designing and Presenting Arguments

Chapter 14: Designing Arguments

When beginning discussion of the material in this chapter, you may want to briefly review with your students the discussion of textual rhetorical analysis and contextual rhetorical analysis in Chapter 5. While visual design can be talked about in terms of ethical, pathetic, and logical appeals, it also can be talked about in terms of context. Ask your students how the context of a given argument often determines the visual form it will take; for example, what argument would two images make together—an image of a politician in front of a poster featuring Uncle Sam—that neither would make alone?

It is likely that your students will not have thought extensively or critically about electronic resources. Encourage them to begin thinking about the ways that word processors and other kinds of software allow them to modify and design their documents. For example, how do tables, charts, and columns aid them in making effective arguments? You may want to review with your students the discussion in Chapter 6 about the visual presentation of data.

IN-CLASS ACTIVITIES

• Bring to class several advertisements or have students find advertisements as a homework assignment and bring to class. Divide the class into small groups of students and ask each group to prepare an analysis of the advertisements. Ask the students to answer the following questions: Who is the audience for each ad? What is each ad's central claim? How does the visual design aid in (or detract from) the ad's ability to make that claim effectively? Do the visual features work well together (and constitute a theme) or do they create confusion? Is there too much *contrast* among and between the visual features? Should there be more *consis-*

tency between and among the visual items. Alternatively, is there too much consistency in the design, so much so that the ad is boring? Are the font size and style effective or do they seem to work against the argument?

• Bring to class examples of misleading visual elements such as charts, graphs, and tables. You might also bring in some examples of photographs that are used in misleading ways, such as those featured in supermarket tabloids or celebrity magazines. As a class, discuss how the visual presentation of the information in these examples can lead to misinterpretation. Discuss also the ethical problems involved in such misrepresentation. Break the students into small groups and have them revise the charts, graphs, or tables to make them less misleading.

• If you are working in a computer-assisted classroom, ask the students to evaluate the first pages of several Web sites. Ask them to choose between 2–4 Web sites that they are familiar with, or that they regularly visit. Which Web site is the most organized in its presentation of information? Why? Which Web site is the least well organized? Why? Does the first page offer too little information or too much information? Is the visual theme unclear? How could it be made clearer? Does each of the visual items on the page have a strong relationship with the other visual items? If not, what visual items would you delete or replace with different content?

SHORT ASSIGNMENTS

• Find a newsletter or brochure that has very little visual appeal. Bring copies of the document to class and have students redesign it according to the principles in this chapter. They might even take samples of their work back to the company or organization from which they got the newsletter or brochure. (This assignment might be made into a larger project, in which students identify an organization for which they will do some volunteer design work. Students might then work in conjunction with the organization to design effective promotional materials.)

• Have your students choose a forum thread on edwardtufte.com relevant to information design, and write a 200-word summary of the posts there.

Then, have the students present their summaries to the class, and discuss the connection between the online discussion and Faigley and Selzer's discussions of document design.

• Ask your students to write a resume while covering material in this chapter. Resumes require that students become familiar with the formatting and design capabilities of word processors, and think carefully about the arrangement, consistency, and contrast of information on a page. Have students consider their ethos. (How do they want to present themselves in the resume?) Have them consider their audience. (What strategies should they employ when laying out the resume? What information should they include, and which is the most important? How should they design the document accordingly?) Teachers have had great results with this assignment in the past. One teacher's student used her resume in a job application and not only got the job but was told that she was hired on the strength of her resume alone!

• Have students find sections in *Good Reasons* that provide information that can be presented graphically and have them design visuals to present this information. They might consider creating charts, tables, diagrams, graphs, maps, or illustrations of some kind. They might also look at the readings in the book to find an argument that would be better served by having some of its information presented graphically.

• Have students complete a rhetorical analysis of a CD's liner notes. Who's the audience? What sort of image is the design meant to portray? Is the design effective or ineffective? Why?

• Provide students with a large amount of data, perhaps from an almanac or a census report. As a homework assignment, have them present the data in a visually effective and organized manner. You might even assign students to make particular arguments with their visual presentation of the data. For instance, you might give your students data regarding the demographics of your home institution. Have some students present the data in a way that *emphasizes* the diversity of your campus population. Have other students present the data in a way that *de-emphasizes* campus diversity.

Chapter 15: Presenting Arguments

Oral arguments are quite different from arguments that appear in the form of a written or visual text. Thus, to begin your discussion of oral presentations, ask the students to think about how they would present a full length written essay orally, and what they think some of the differences are between a strong written presentation and a strong oral presentation. Ask them what the constraints of each medium are. If the students are having difficulty identifying these differences or these constraints, prompt them by pointing to 1–2. Point out, for example, that in order to make an oral presentation effective, speakers often have to consciously modulate their normal speaking voice. They slow their words down if their speech is normally very rapid. If their normal speaking voice is not loud, they consciously raise the volume of their voice when they speak to an audience. An example of a difference between an oral and a written argument is that in an oral presentation, the audience does not have the advantage of turning back the "pages" of the speaker's text in order to review an earlier point that was made. Therefore, speakers often repeat the main points of their arguments throughout their oral presentations. In written arguments the main points often appear only in the opening and concluding paragraphs. Also, oral presentations typically rely more on visual aids than do most written arguments. If audio-visual equipment or an AV equipped room is unavailable, a speaker can use printed handouts to keep the main points of his or her argument always present before the eyes of the audience.

Ask your students what else speakers do to make their oral presentations effective. Ask them about teachers they have had. Why were some particularly effective when presenting information in class? Why did they think some of their teachers were particularly ineffective even though they also knew that the teachers were experts in the given subject (perhaps even authors of books on the given subject)? Ask them if different subjects require different presentation strategies? That is, could a successful algebra teacher use similar teaching strategies in an English class?

IN-CLASS ACTIVITIES

• Focus and time-management are crucial when giving oral presentations. This activity provides one way of making this point. Break students into groups of 2–3 and provide each group with the same collection of information (e.g., a series of articles and letters to the editor about a particular issue, or several different articles and reviews about one movie or album). Explain to the groups that each needs to prepare a five-minute, a ten-minute, and a fifteen-minute presentation in which they summarize the material you've provided them. Give students time in class to complete the assignment (or make it a homework assignment). Then, at your next class meeting, randomly select several groups to make one of their presentations. Time each presentation and have the class as a whole discuss how effective the groups were at managing their time and developing a focused, persuasive argument.

• Find the transcribed text of an oral presentation (americanrhetoric.com is a good source for such transcripts) and have your students compare it to an essay written for print (see if you can find examples of each by the same author). What are the differences between the two? How many of those differences can be attributed to the differences between writing for a speaker and writing for print? You might also want to have two students read each essay out-loud for the purpose of further comparison between their oral and written features.

SHORT ASSIGNMENTS

• Have students (individually or in groups) interview one of their teachers. Have them ask the teacher questions about his or her rhetorical strategies. How does the teacher organize his or her lectures in order to communicate effectively? What does he or she strive for when designing class handouts? Does the teacher maintain a Web site? If so, how has he or she designed it to be an effective tool for communication and pedagogy?

• Have students take a paper they wrote earlier in the semester and make a plan for transforming it into an oral presentation. What kind of presentation should it be (e.g., a persuasive speech, an informative speech, an entertaining speech)? How will their audience shape the way that they make their presentation? Will they need to change their reasons or evidence for the purpose of the presentation? Will they need to change the order in which they present their argument? Will they need to change their opener or closer (adding humor, perhaps)? Will they require visual aids that they did not use in the paper? Students should use the principles we outline in this chapter to guide them in their work.

• You might expand this assignment so that students have the opportunity not only to transform an earlier paper into an oral presentation but also to revise and sharpen their argument in the process. Or, you might have students exchange papers, transforming one of their peers' papers into an oral presentation. If you decide to have the students present in class, you might ask students to develop (as a homework assignment) a standard form or checklist with which the class can assess the presentations. Again, students should use the principles in this chapter to guide them in their work.

Part 5: Researching Arguments

Chapter 16: Planning Research

Part 5 of *Good Reasons with Contemporary Arguments* can be taught most effectively in conjunction with one or several essay assignments that require research.

We strongly recommend that you teach research methods as deliberately as you do the writing process. Unfortunately, you cannot assume that your students will have research skills when they arrive in your class, so it's best to cover all aspects of research in your course. With first-semester freshmen—and even with upperclassmen—it is usually necessary to spend several class days at the library, learning about available resources and where they can be found, asking the reference librarians questions, and developing specific strategies for research. Students are not likely to find this approach patronizing or a waste of their time. Rather, you will frequently hear that this hands-on experience will open the library to your students, and that they will feel much more comfortable there after completing this unit.

Faigley and Selzer devote a significant portion of Chapter 16 to the collection of primary source material like personal interviews and surveys. If these methods of research are appropriate to the types of papers you will assign in your class, try to encourage your students to make use of them. However, keep in mind that monitoring and evaluating this kind of research can be more challenging than monitoring and evaluating traditional library research. If your students decide to conduct interviews or distribute surveys, devote some time in class to helping them brainstorm interview questions and prepare their surveys, then provide opportunities for them to improve their skill at these activities as the semester progresses.

IN-CLASS ACTIVITIES

• Return to an earlier assignment where you had students brainstorm topics (see p. 43 for an example). After your discussion of the types of research introduced in this chapter, select a few of the topics that the students suggested and have them brainstorm different kinds of research—library research or interviews, for example—that would provide the best reasons and evidence to support an argument about that topic.

• Encourage your students to use the invention exercises mentioned in Chapter 4 to help them generate research topics, questions, and possible sources. For example, as a class you could brainstorm topics that are relevant to the student body at your school, or to the local community; individually, you could have your students freewrite on topic ideas for 5–7 minutes in class, then share those ideas with the group.

SHORT ASSIGNMENTS

• Have students compile an annotated list of the general research resources at your school. Start by developing a list of 30 or 40 print and online resources (such a list may already be available from the English or Communications librarian at your school) and assign 2–3 to each student. Have students write a descriptive summary of the resources they've been assigned, noting for each one its audience, breadth, and general subject matter along with the kinds of information it contains, what group or individuals publish it, which students generally use it, and why. Encourage students to ask librarians to help them answer these questions. Have the students bring copies of their reports for everyone in the class or post them to a course Web site. Alternatively, you can compile the reports yourself and make the complete report available to the class.

Chapter 17: Finding Sources

Discussions of keyword searching and annotated lists of academic databases can be dry stuff for students to absorb if they are not able to test these resources in a hands-on manner. If at all possible, discuss these chapters with your students in a computer lab or classroom where they have access to a computer. If you do not teach in a computer assisted classroom, your school (or the library itself) may have a computer lab that you can reserve for your class. If that is not possible, have your discussion of this material coincide with your library visit, where you can demonstrate the principles and techniques mentioned here at a search terminal.

Additionally, you might contact your school library to see if orientation sessions are offered. If you teach at a larger school, it is likely that there is a dedicated library for the humanities, or that your library has librarians who deal exclusively with the humanities, English, or Communication Studies who would be wiling to introduce your students to the library resources available for these disciplines. At smaller schools, your library's reference librarian can do the same. If you make an effort to foster a relationship with the library staff, you will find that they are generally willing to help your students become acquainted with the research resources available to them.

IN-CLASS ACTIVITIES

• Choose a topic relevant to the class, and have your students, either individually or in small groups, brainstorm a list of keywords to use when searching for information on that topic. Have the individuals or groups present their results to the rest of the class, and, as a group, rank the keywords from most to least relevant. Then, if there is time and you have access to computers, search through a few resources—like an Internet search engine or academic database—using those keywords and evaluate the results. Do these searches suggest that the keywords chosen by the group are good ones? Do they suggest different or additional keywords? Modify the group's list as necessary.

SHORT ASSIGNMENTS

• Repeat the resource annotation assignment from page 68, only this time have the list of resources consist of only electronic databases to which your school subscribes. If your university subscribes to only a few of these databases, have each group interact with each database. Students often rely solely on Internet search engines when doing research, and this exercise will give them some experience and familiarity with specialized search resources.

Chapter 18: Evaluating and Recording Sources

You will most likely find that your students are highly skilled at searching the Internet and evaluating the sources they find there. One way of approaching this material is to show how skills they already possess can be translated to similar tasks in different environments. For example, when searching the Internet for a topic of interest to them, they will most likely already know enough of the language of that topic to find what they are looking for. If they are interested in finding reviews for restaurants in Springfield, they will have to provide additional keywords— Springfield, MO? Springfield, MA? restaurants that serve breakfast?—to narrow their search. Using examples like this one, demonstrate how they can use subject lists in specialized databases to learn the language of that database to appropriately narrow searches in those environments. Similarly, when searching for restaurants, they already know that the phrase "the best Mexican food in Springfield!" means something quite different when it is posted on a restaurant's home page than when it is posted on an independent review site. In short, if you make use of your students' current expertise in searching for and evaluating sources, you will likely find that they pick up on the material in these chapters much more quickly than they otherwise would have.

IN-CLASS ACTIVITIES

• Choose 2–3 keywords relevant to a recent class discussion or assignment. Divide your students into groups of 2–3, and have each group search for that keyword using a different resource (an Internet search engine, an academic database, a Web directory, and so on). Have each group perform a quick evaluation of the first two results of the search and present their findings to the class. What differences exist in the search results conducted using these different resources?

• Students will likely need some help when you begin talking about source evaluation, so bring several different kinds of sources (journals and books, print and online) to class and, as a group, model the evaluation methods discussed in this chapter. Stress that sources are not uniformly *good* or *bad*. Rather, some are better suited to particular projects than others. Emphasize the connection of sources to the rhetorical appeals. For example, have them ask: how will the use of this source affect my ethos as an author?

• With your students, develop a worksheet that they may use when assessing the sources they plan to use in their research projects. Follow the guidelines listed in the "Evaluating Sources" section of this chapter when developing your worksheet. Make copies of the worksheet for everyone in the class, or provide an electronic copy on your course Web site for students to access later.

SHORT ASSIGNMENTS

• Prepare a list of ten different Web sites addressing one particular topic (e.g., global warming, animal rights, display of the confederate flag) and have your students assess whether those sources would be considered credible in an academic essay. To complete their assignment, have students use the criteria for evaluating print and Web sources in Chapter 18.

• Have your students read Paul Duguid's article "Inheritance and Loss? A Brief Survey of Google Books." After reading and discussing the article, direct your students to select a book from the library written before the twentieth century (books printed before 1923 are generally in the public domain and are therefore likely to be available online for free), and compare that book with its digital counterpart, either in Google Books or in the Internet Archive (archive.org). They will not need to read the entirety of each version of the book; rather, have them select pages and sections from each as Duguid does with *Tristram Shandy*. Have them briefly present their findings to the rest of the class. What do their findings suggest about the reliability of online book sources?

Chapter 19: Writing the Research Paper

Generally, students taking introductory composition courses struggle with selecting the right quotations, working sources and quotations smoothly into their prose, and using attributive tags. They will have heard about plagiarism before, but many of them will not feel confident in making distinctions between what counts as plagiarism and what does not. Be open about what your students need to learn. Explain to them that most beginning college students struggle with the skills mentioned here, and that you will be working on these skills throughout the term.

Introduce the use of sources and documentation in terms of rhetorical effectiveness, particularly in terms of ethos. How does the choice of sources and effective documentation affect the ethos of the writer? For instance, what's the difference between noting that the *New York Times* has conducted a survey that produced results to support your argument, and that "a newspaper" has produced results that support your argument? Students should announce the credibility of their sources when they can.

Even though your students will have likely written research papers before taking your class, it is also likely that they still struggle with the language and structure of academic arguments. Be sure to spend time in class reviewing the bullets in the "Incorporate Quotations" section of this chapter, making sure to point out the opportunities to expand their critical vocabulary that it provides them.

Covering intellectual property and plagiarism, you will want to emphasize the seriousness of the problem without making students afraid to use sources. In our experience, students rarely intend to copy sources without attribution. Those that make mistakes in citing sources generally do so because they have not yet learned how to paraphrase, cite, and quote from sources correctly. We recommend that you have students complete several exercises in which they paraphrase and summarize the central argument of a source. You should also explain that plagiarism is often the result of incomplete research. Often we feel compelled to use the language of others when we don't feel confident or qualified enough to speak about a subject on our own. Your students will have a number of questions about plagiarism. Again, handle them in a way that emphasizes the seriousness of the issue but that does not make it seem like the *only* issue when dealing with sources. We recommend that you first attempt to work with those students who go beyond the limits of what is acceptable regarding the use of intellectual property. Of course, if these students continue to break the rules, you should take appropriate action.

Also, be sure to emphasize the importance of good research *habits* as your students prepare to write their research papers. Typically, many instances of inadvertent plagiarism can be avoided if the student either makes careful notes on the source material, or makes clear distinctions between his or her own summaries of the source and the direct text of the source. You might find it helpful to require your students to prepare notecards on all the sources they use, or to use bookmarking services like del.icio.us or StumbleUpon (stumbleupon.com) to keep track of their online sources. Above all, stress to them the importance of noting all the sources they examine, not just the ones they think they will use. If they do only the latter, they will find that when it comes time to write their paper, they will invariably want to use a source that they had previously passed over, and they will waste time attempting to find that source again, time that could have been saved by simply making a note of the source the first time they saw it.

IN-CLASS ACTIVITIES

• Bring to class copies of articles from several different disciplines and discuss how each distinguishes between "common knowledge" and information that needs to be documented.

• Distribute an editorial in class and have students paraphrase it in 50 words or less. Emphasize that they have learned skills all semester that should help them in this activity. Also emphasize that in order to paraphrase a persuasive piece of writing they need to summarize both its central claim and reasons, perhaps also noting both its audience and evidence.

• Have your students experiment with bookmarking services like del.icio.us, Furl (furl.net), or StumbleUpon (stumbleupon.com) for keeping track of online sources (students will have to create accounts on these sites, but those accounts are free). Repeat the keyword-searching exercise on page 71, but this time have your students record and annotate their results in one of these bookmarking services. When they are finished, have them share their results either by email or through the course Web site. (Note: For this activity, you will need to limit searches to Web resources like Ask.com and Google Academic because many library databases do not provide permanent URLs for their pages and therefore cannot be linked to.)

• Have students bring in a short section of one of their papers that presents an argument supported by a quotation (probably a paragraph or so). Have them randomly choose three verbs from the section "Verbs that Introduce Quotations and Paraphrases" and replace the attributive language in their paragraph with those verbs. Then have volunteers share their rewrites with the class. Although in some cases the passage will seem virtually unchanged, in others you will likely end up with examples that make little sense or which completely change the meaning of the original passage. Use these examples to point out that, even when words mean something similar, they can have subtle differences that completely alter the meaning or tone of an argument. Encourage your students to consult the list of verbs when they are revising, in order to find those that are most effective for their arguments.

SHORT ASSIGNMENTS

• Have students trade 2–3 pages from essays that they are currently writing and assess their peers' use of sources. Are the sources appropriate to the argument and rhetorical context? Are they effectively used? Are quotations effectively integrated into the paper's prose? Are the sources correctly cited?

• Have students find a Web site in which sources are *not* used or cited effectively. Have them bring a hard copy of the site in to class and then explain how the author might have used sources more effectively.

• While your students are working on their research projects, direct them to choose a few sentences to paraphrase from one of their sources. Select a few students to share their work with the class, showing both the original text and their paraphrase (if your classroom does not have access to an overhead projector, require students to bring copies of their work and the relevant section of the source for everyone). As a class, compare the original text with the paraphrase, and use these comparisons to discuss what makes a paraphrase effective and what constitutes plagiarism in a paraphrase. (Note: It is best to view this exercise as simply that: an exercise. Some of your students will still be learning how to paraphrase a source without plagiarizing it, so it is likely to be counterproductive to that learning if you put on your Plagiarism Police hat and condemn them in this setting. Rather, praise good examples, and point out where less good examples cross the line from paraphrase into plagiarism, stressing that this kind of line crossing needs to be corrected before students turn in their major assignments.)

Chapters 20–21: MLA and APA Documentation

It is crucial that students learn that they can answer many of their questions about document formats by consulting handbooks such as *Good Reasons*. In responding to a first draft, there is no need for you to correct every error of documentation (though you should mark those places where a student runs the risk of plagiarism). Simply tell the student that the documentation is not correctly formatted and that it is their responsibility to correct those errors in their final draft. By doing this, you require the students to consult their handbooks—a practice that will serve them well in the future.

WITKOWSKI, "NEED A CURE FOR TRIBE FEVER? HOW ABOUT A DIP IN THE LAKE?"

1. What is Witkowski's central claim? What is his purpose in making this argument?
2. What are the reasons that Witkowski uses to support his claim? In other words, how does he justify his solution to the controversy over the Cleveland Indians' Chief Wahoo logo?
3. Are Witkowski's reasons good reasons? Why or why not?
4. What is the structure of Witkowski's argument? Is the structure effective? Why or why not? How does the structure affect Witkowski's credibility?
5. If Witkowski's proposal (to change the name of the Cleveland Indians to the Cleveland Lakers) is accepted, what will it primarily achieve? Will it primarily help to eliminate racial prejudice against Native American Indians and their culture? Will it primarily help to do something else?
6. What is the context of Witkowski's argument? Who is his target audience? In what larger social and cultural conversations does his essay participate? To what larger social and cultural conversations does his essay contribute?

IN-CLASS ACTIVITIES

• Distribute information or ideas drawn from several different sources and have students incorporate the material into a unified paragraph. Make sure they handle quotations effectively and cite their sources correctly according to either MLA or APA style.

SHORT ASSIGNMENTS

• Have students interview a more advanced student majoring in the field in which they expect to major. Have them ask the older student about the citation style that is standard in their field and the print and online resources to which the older student most often turns. Have your students report on their findings to the rest of the class.

• As part of their research assignment, have students prepare note cards documenting the bibliographical information from 10 unique sources, as well as some sort of annotation of the importance of each source—either a summary, paraphrase, or quotation that they find useful.

Part 6: Contemporary Arguments

Chapter 22: Negotiating the Environment

This chapter contains a range of arguments—definitional, causal, evaluative, narrative—on a topic that remains one of the most important political issues of the day: the environment.

Perhaps the best way of using this chapter as a unit (as opposed to using
just a few of the readings) is to compare how the authors collected here
write about the natural world. How does each define the term "environment"? What does each assume to be "natural"? And how does each take
advantage of a distinctive style? For example, E. O. Wilson writes about
humanity's responsibility to the natural world in generally abstract terms,
Wendell Berry grounds his argument in the details of a poem, and Al
Gore presents his argument in the form of a slide presentation—does
each author develop a style appropriate to the context in which she or he
writes?

Finally, it may be helpful for you and your students to note that this
chapter does not take a pro-environmental stance for granted. Horner and
Williams argue against pro-global warming and pro-ecological arguments made by scientists and the environmental lobby—and in so doing,
calls those arguments into question.

WILSON, "THE CONSERVATION ETHIC"

Wilson's essay is a broad look at ethics in relation to the environment.
He suggests a pattern for people's questions—they go from ethical, to
informational, then back to ethical as knowledge is increased. Wilson
does definitional work for both "ethics" and "environment." He focuses
on issues of species diversity in talking about the environment.

You will note some excerpts from Aldo Leopold's "The Land Ethic" situated below a portion of Wilson's article. Wilson calls on Leopold for his definition of ethics, and the excerpts from this text can be used for direct comparison and contrast with Wilson. The Leopold excerpts may be particularly useful for exploring with your students how one author can use the ideas of another as a launching pad for his or her own argument, without necessarily disagreeing with that author.

Wilson seeks a "deepening of the conservation ethic," and says it requires an evolutionary view that can consider consequences across greater spans of time than just one's own life or even a few generations. Wilson points out that the worst thing humans are probably doing is destroying natural habitats, an activity that humans have it within their power to stop. He argues that each newly extinct species (including the insects he has spent his life studying) can have huge negative ramifications for the possibilities and well-being of other species with whom they share a habitat.

1. How does Wilson expand on or disagree with the short excerpts from Leopold's work? What definitions do they have in common? What ethical principles does each work from? How do they support or argue for those basic ethical principles?
2. Ask your students what environmental issues struck them as most important before reading Wilson's article. How do they (the students) think about the environment in ethical terms? Has Wilson influenced the issues they think are most vital? What about the article contributed to this possible influence? What definitions in the article did they have the most trouble with or wish to challenge? Environmental issues often are good for talking about stasis points, where a key thing to figure out is whether the differences are about definitions, facts, the quality of something, or what to do. Which of these areas seems most important for any rebuttal of Wilson?
3. Where does the environment fit into students' hierarchies of values? How do long and short time scales impact what one values most? Wilson discusses the need for a longer ethical view, but it can often be difficult to inspire actions based on events that will occur in the distant future. What rhetorical tactics might specifically help address this time issue?

MOMADAY, "THE WAY TO RAINY MOUNTAIN"

Momaday uses his Kiowa heritage to accomplish a number of objectives in this excerpt. Primarily, he expresses a sense of necessity: when one comes from a particular heritage, he says, one is obligated to do and say and value certain things. Moreover, he suggests, one is tied to the land. The "land" here is not just the land expressed as a general term, in the way that Leopold uses it, but a particular piece of land, a particular region with particular natural features, grasses, plants, animals, underneath a particular patch of sky.

Compared with Wilson, Momaday's essay is less general and more particular. It is not a persuasive essay about the need for environmental conservation or the hyperbole of environmentalist rhetoric; it does not contribute to the public debate about the "environment" or "nature" in any immediate way. But it dos express *why* the land is important to an individual and to particular groups of people. Certainly, Momaday would assert that nature must be viewed as a system in which all the parts contribute and have an equal right to be treated with dignity. But convincing us of this is not his concern.

Rather, he wants us to understand how his people, the Kiowas, are a part of a particular landscape. Rainy Mountain is the central image here, but Momaday is not urging us to preserve individual monuments. The monuments—Rainy Mountain in Oklahoma, Devil's Tower in Wyoming, Palo Duro Canyon in Texas—are merely the symbolic manifestations of nature as a system. And the people of that region are entirely implicated in that system.

1. How might Momaday respond to E. O. Wilson's ideas about restructuring the terms of our debate about the environment? Momaday is largely concerned here with the particulars of his Oklahoma region, but would he agree with Wilson's larger claims? How might he disagree with Wilson's points?

2. The "Native American" point of view about the environment has been portrayed many times in recent years, but rarely by Native Americans. Often, self-appointed spokespeople claim to speak from a Native American perspective or with an understanding of Native American philosophy. Ask the students to discuss what images or

stereotypes they have about Native Americans and the environment, and ask them to think about where these ideas come from. What is the difference between having one's ideas portrayed by others and being able to express those ideas oneself? What problems can arise in the translation between the source and the portrayer?

3. What audience does Momaday have in mind for this piece? How do his strategies reflect that audience (or audiences)?

BULLARD, "HOW RACE AFFECTED THE FEDERAL GOVERNMENT'S RESPONSE TO KATRINA"

In this speech, Robert Bullard mentions a number of cases where the government's response to disasters—terrorism or natural disasters—seems to have been different in areas where the population consists primarily of minorities. According to Bullard, the government's response to Katrina is merely symptomatic of a pattern of neglect.

1. What is Bullard's main claim? What evidence does he give to support that claim?

2. Have your students outline Bullard's case for the U.S. government's habitual disregard for African-American populations during crisis situations. Do they find this case credible? Compare it to Kanye West's statement after Hurricane Katrina that "George Bush doesn't care about black people." Is this claim compelling in light of the evidence that Bullard complies in this talk?

3. What kind of audience does Bullard's talk seem to be addressed to? An affluent, middle-class one? A disadvantaged one? African-American? Caucasian? If the argument had to be tailored to a different group, how could that be done?

WENDELL BERRY, "MANIFESTO: THE MAD FARMER LIBERATION FRONT"

Many of Wendell Berry's poems are set in rural, farming, or wooded areas. "Manifesto: The Mad Farmer Liberation Front" has anti-technology and anti-modernist themes. Berry attempts to show a larger time scale with the fifth and sixth stanzas, not unlike Wilson's earlier argument. His poem speaks directly to someone, almost entirely in the imperative. Berry's argument in the first two stanzas describes a condition that he assumes one should avoid. He then spends much of the rest of the poem delivering statements about how to act to avoid that condition where "Not even your future will be a mystery" and "Your mind will be . . . shut away in a little drawer." Many of his suggestions about how to live involve valuing things commonly considered "natural." Those include trees, carrion, humus, birth processes, and fields. His imagery opposes natural elements to the bureaucracy and desires of modernity.

1. It is not always common to think of a poem as an argument. How is this poem an argument? What does it argue for and against? What conversation might it be participating in?
2. Why is this poem included in the environment section of a book? Do you think it should be? What is it saying about the environment?
3. What serves as evidence in this argument? Does the imagery work to convince an audience in some way? Where can you identify both logos and pathos in Berry's poem?
4. How does Berry's understanding of time in relation to the environment compare with E. O. Wilson's "evolutionary time"?

ISSUE IN FOCUS: CLIMATE CHANGE

The "Issues in Focus" sections of *Good Reasons with Contemporary Arguments* are designed to give several brief arguments, all on a specific topic. Some arguments will respond directly to each other, while most will simply be different perspectives on a small issue.

The essays in this "in Focus" section outline several different approaches to the topic of climate change. As Faigley and Selzer point out, debates over climate change—popularly known as global warming—have received a great deal of press over the past few years. Your students are likely to be familiar with the broad outlines of the climate debate and the names of major proponents for competing climate theories; they may even have heard of climate treaties like the Kyoto Protocol. However, it is similarly likely that many of them will not have read or engaged in any serious debate over the subject. For this reason, your discussion of the readings contained in this section will be an excellent opportunity for them to practice using good reasons when debating questions in a public forum.

Due to its politicization, climate change is a polarizing subject in the United States. In light of this fact, you may need to spend extra time in class ensuring that your students resist knee-jerk reactions to the arguments here and instead carefully consider the claims and reasons provided by each author. As with other controversial subjects, it may be helpful to frame your discussion of climate change in terms of the argumentation guidelines provided by Faigley and Selzer, rather than in terms of absolutes.

GORE, "WHAT IS GLOBAL WARMING?" AND "TEN THINGS TO DO TO HELP STOP GLOBAL WARMING"

These two short pieces by former Vice President Al Gore outline his appeal for greater awareness of global warming as well as actions that individuals can take to counteract this climate trend. Both texts follow unique formats. The first is similar to a slide presentation, like his famous presentation in the film *An Inconvenient Truth*, while the second is merely a short list. When discussing these selections with your students, you may be interested in exploring their responses to these non-traditional formats.

1. What is Gore's argument? What evidence does he use to support that argument?
2. Unlike some of the other articles in this chapter, Gore provides references for his claims. How does this affect the impact of his argument?
3. How do the images affect your reception of the article? While Gore provides detailed references for his claims, he doesn't provide any context for these images. Do they detract from or add to his argument?

HORNER, "TOP TEN 'GLOBAL-WARMING' MYTHS"

As with Gore's second text, Horner's "Top Ten 'Global-Warming' Myths" takes the form of a list. In it, he outlines what are, according to him, erroneous claims made by those who argue that global warming is a serious problem that demands an immediate response. This technique—anticipating an argument contrary to your own position in order to rebut it—is sometimes called "prolepsis." In Horner's text, it is not always clear who is responsible for the "myths" he is rebutting. While some of his points are direct responses to Gore's arguments, for example "The science is settled—CO_2 causes global warming" others are attributed to more general entities like global warming "alarmists," as with "Global warming means more frequent, more severe storms."

1. What is Horner's argument? What evidence does he use to support that argument?
2. Compare Horner's claims and use of evidence to that of Gore: how are they different? Which is more effective? More persuasive? Why?
3. How would you characterize Horner's tone in this essay?
4. Each of Horner's points begins with a " 'Global Warming' Myth." What is the source of these myths? Global warming activists? Scientists? Does it matter?

McCoy, "And Looking at Our Extended Forecast"

In this editorial cartoon, a weatherman provides an "extended forecast," not of the next few days or the next week, but of the "next several decades."

1. What is the argument being made in this cartoon? What evidence supports that argument?
2. How would the argument of this cartoon be different without the labels ("current science")? Could its meaning be altered by changing these labels?
3. What cultural structures does the joke of the cartoon depend on? How does equating weather science with television meteorologists help (or hinder) McCoy's argument?

JENKINS, "BURNING AT THE STAKE"

While Gore and Horner focus on how global warming will (or will not) affect the world climate, Jenkins focuses on a more specific region of the globe, the area surrounding the equator. According to Jenkins, this 46-degree-wide belt will be severely impacted by global warming, and one of the results of this climate change will be increased violence directed against religious groups, as the privation and hardships caused by global warming cause people to look for scapegoats to blame for their problems.

1. What is Jenkins's argument, and what evidence does he use to support it?
2. Who is the audience(s) for this article? Why is Jenkins directing this argument to this particular audience(s)? Is there a religious imperative to respond to global warming?
3. How would it change the effect of this argument for American audiences if it was about Muslims rather than Christians? Mormons?

WILLIAMS, "BUYING INTO THE GREEN MOVEMENT"

Williams argues that consumers are being seduced by the marketing of "green"—or environmentally friendly—products into a "Snack Well's moment" where feelings of having done good by the environment with a green purchase will encourage wasteful behaviors that will cancel out or even counteract that good. This problem has led to a debate in the environmental community over the value of green consumption and its true impact on the environment.

1. What is Williams's argument, and what evidence does he use to support that argument?
2. How do your students respond to the connection between economics and ecology? Does this connection damage the "ethos" of pro-ecological arguments?
3. What is the more balanced view of environmentalism that Williams concludes his essay with? Is it more or less persuasive than the one he challenges?

CHICAGO TRIBUNE, "FAST CLOTHES VS. GREEN CLOTHES"; AND
ROSENTHAL, "ENVIRONMENTALLY UNFRIENDLY TREND: FAST FASH-
ION"; AND "HOW 'GREEN' IS YOUR T-SHIRT?"

These two articles and the sidebar all deal with the environmental impact
of clothing choices. They make as their target "fast" clothes that are designed and made cheaply, and which quickly go out of fashion, forcing
an endless cycle of new clothing manufacturing which taxes the environment both by increasing the polluting byproducts of farming and bur-
dening landfills with yesterday's couture.

1. What is the argument in this editorial? What evidence is used to support it?
2. What is Rosenthal's argument? How does she support it?
3. Compare the two short essays: how are they the same (in argument,
   style, tone, audience)? How are they different? Is one more compelling than the other? If so, why?
4. How does the table in the box How "Green" Is Your T-Shirt? depict-
   ing the energy usage required by cotton and polyester clothing affect
   your own decisions about purchasing garments? How does the table
   format help or hinder this argument?
5. Can the data in the Chicago *Tribune* and Rosenthal essays be con-
   verted into tabular form? Into some other kind of data graphic, like a
   pie or bar chart? If it was presented in this format, would it help or
   hinder the arguments of those essays?

IN-CLASS ACTIVITIES

• Have students consider their own ethical systems and values. Have
them try applying their own ethical views to the issues of species extinc-
tion and biodiversity that Wilson discusses. Then have students reflect on
any differences in values they have with Wilson and how those values
lead to different sorts of actions.

• Have students explore their own relationship to the land of their families. How does their family view the land? Many, perhaps most, students
will have a difficult time relating to Momaday's connection with his
Oklahoma homeland and may choose to see his feelings as an "Indian

thing"—encourage these students to think about the area or region from which their family comes, whether it be a farm in the Midwest or a small village in Lithuania. How have the traditions and the natural setting of that place been transmitted through their family histories? Have students write a narrative argument based on their experiences. Encourage students to think about how their own experiences connect to the issues raised by the essays in this section.

• Summarize Momaday's essay so that his central claim and reasons—that is, the logical structure of his argument—is absolutely clear.

• Based on the assumption that Bullard's argument is correct, have your students write proposal essays that outline plans for rectifying the government's inadequate response to disasters for disadvantaged groups.

• Pick one stanza from Berry's poem. Discuss how it does and does not argue for a form of environmentalism. Identify some of the values assumed by the imperative commands to the audience in that stanza.

• Divide your students in half, then break each half into groups of 2–3. Have one half of the students identify a group that is typically opposed to the idea of global warming and then outline an argument that shows the exigence of combating global warming for that group, as Jenkins does with Christians. Have the other half repeat this exercise, yet have them choose groups that are pro-global warming and outline arguments that show how this stance is harmful to that group.

SHORT ASSIGNMENTS

• Wilson's article makes specific use of Aldo Leopold's work, but goes well beyond it into new territory. Have students take a key point from Wilson's article and not simply agree or disagree with it, but use it as a starting point for an idea of their own.

• Wilson makes use of hypothetical scenarios to make his points more compelling. Have students describe an environmental (or other) scenario that makes a case for a particular type of environmental (in)action.

• Momaday's essay gives students an alternate model of persuasive writing. It makes a "point," but does not do so by using the strict models of academic writing. Suggest that students write a persuasive argument about the environment in which the central claim and reasons are carried by the force of a story—either a story, like Momaday's, rooted in the author's own experience, or a more journalistic story.

• Have your students research images of Rainy Mountain, Devil's Tower, Palo Duro Canyon on the Web. Then, using Momaday's essay for context, have them write short visual analyses of 2–3 images they find.

• Have students pick a natural disaster and research the response to that disaster for various racial and economic groups. They will probably need to find archives of local papers through your campus library to do this well.

• Have your students perform a visual analysis of the images in Gore's first article. What is their role in his argument? Compare Gore's use of images with that of Horner. How are they different? Why are they different?

• Gore and Berry's arguments are styled quite differently from the other essays in this text. Have your students write about the style and form of these two articles. How would it change the effect of these articles if they were written like a traditional essay? Presented in as a slideshow?

• Write a poem that serves as an argument. Then write a short analysis of how the poem works as both a poem and argument. Or, write a short prose argument, then take the same point and put it into poetic form.

Chapter 23: Confronting Sexual Difference

The murder of University of Wyoming student Matthew Shepard, Vermont and Hawaii's "domestic partner" or "civil union" legislation, the popularity of television shows such as *Will and Grace* and *Six Feet Under*; these and many other recent events have brought issues relating to gay rights and homosexuality more to the center of public debate than they ever have been. And the terms of the debate are changing: where once, the central question was what to "do" with homosexuals, now the presence of gay people is taken for granted, even in such unlikely places as the Republican Party (via the Log Cabin Republicans, a group of gay GOP members) and religious institutions. The issues have become more practical and workaday—what is the relation between a gay partnership and a marriage? To what degree should the presence of gay people in the most intimate and stressful areas of daily life be accepted? But the old issues remain, as Peter Gomes reminds us: there are still many people, no matter how much the culture as a whole moves toward acceptance of gay people, who view homosexuality as a sin and an abomination. Students may recall that, on September 11, 2001, Jerry Falwell claimed that God may have allowed the terrorist attacks on America because the nation was currently experiencing a period of moral decay. According to Falwell, gays, lesbians, and feminists in particular shared blame for the attacks.

Students will doubtless have strong feelings about the topics in this unit. You may have a few gay students (closeted or "out") in your class, as well as a few students who feel, unequivocally, that homosexuality is a moral wrong. Dealing with such strong and emotional beliefs can be one of the most difficult tasks a teacher has, but it can also be the most rewarding. Students with strong beliefs—even if you feel that those beliefs are ignorant or dangerous or wrong—have a great deal to teach other students about the energizing effects of commitment. Especially for first-year writers—just emerging from high-school environments in which diversity and/or substantive classroom discussion may have been minimal—an encounter with other students who hold strong beliefs can show them that commitment and conviction can actually motivate learning and provide them with other positive outcomes.

This section also provides an excellent opportunity for you to make connections with the environment chapter, for in both sections many of the writers express deep and unchanging philosophical or religious convictions within the context of discussions over the inherently compromise-oriented realm of public policy. Students can see these debates as examples of how a democracy works: not through adherence to non-negotiable absolutes, but through conversation and give-and-take.

VAZQUEZ, "APPEARANCES"

Vazquez's article melds together at least three forms of argumentation: it is a narrative argument, a causal argument, and a proposal. It is also powerful and heartfelt. She effectively tells the stories of a number of straight people who suffered physical attacks brought on because the attackers thought they were homosexuals, and through those stories uses pathos to get readers to sympathize with the victims of violence. She argues, using anecdotal evidence, that particular conceptual structures of manhood and femininity are responsible for gay-bashing attacks. She also strongly urges straight people to try and overcome these structures of thought and uses of language that end up marginalizing gay people.

But Vazquez writes this piece to appeal to straight people. All the victims whose stories she tells are straight, and she assumes a straight audience when she asks her readers to refrain from using offensive language around friends, children, and coworkers. Students might want to discuss why she chooses this approach, instead of telling any one of the myriad stories of gay people who were attacked and even killed because of their sexuality. Does Vazquez sell her identity short in an attempt to appeal to straight readers? Or is this a canny way to convince straight people who might sympathize less with gay victims of violence?

1. Why does Vazquez say that the people who commit violence against gay people "are in the same psychic prison as their victims"? What is the nature of this "psychic prison," and what does it prevent us from doing?

2. Is homophobia the same kind of "bigotry" as racism or religious prejudice, as Vazquez would have us believe, or does it derive from a different source? What causes bigotry, according to Vazquez? Students might want to suggest other sources for prejudice.

3. In her stories of gay bashing, Vazquez purposefully chooses anecdotes of straight people who are mistaken for gay people. Why? Would her argument be less effective if she told the stories of real gay people—Matthew Shepard, for instance—who suffered anti-gay violence? Does this diminish the force of her argument, or strengthen it?

4. At the end of her essay, Vazquez asserts that "Personhood is imminent." What does she mean by this? In your opinion, what is her definition of "personhood"? And why, if attacks on gay people are increasing, is "personhood" coming closer?

GOMES, "HOMOPHOBIC? READ YOUR BIBLE"

Gomes' article is a fairly straightforward rebuttal of the most common grounds for condemning homosexual behavior: the notion that the Bible specifically prohibits homosexual conduct. Students can use this short piece as a model for rebuttal arguments: Gomes portrays his opponents' views, then re-examines the same evidence from which his opponents derive their views and gives another (and to his mind, more correct) interpretation of this evidence. He argues that "fundamentalists" "'read' Scripture... through the lens of their own prejudices and personal values," and are not paying close enough attention to the actual text of the Bible and its context.

Discussion of this article might lead to a pitched argument in your classroom about how to interpret the Bible. Especially if there are a number of students who are knowledgeable about Scripture, this can be a difficult topic to discuss in class. One strategy for dealing with this kind of conflict is to focus on the method of Gomes' argument, not on its substance. How do we determine the "correct" way of reading a text? What constitutes sufficient evidence for a correct reading when evidence seems to conflict?

1. Gomes alludes to the civil-rights struggle at the end of this essay. Why does he do this? What is the basis for the comparison between the civil-rights struggle and the controversy over Biblical condemnation of homosexuality?
2. Gomes and Sullivan defend homosexuality on very different terms. How does each argue that homosexuality is not harmful? Does either argue that it is a societal good?
3. Gomes writes a simple, straightforward argument that relies heavily on ethos. How does he establish his credibility, and how does his ethos support his rhetorical aim?
4. Does Gomes fairly represent the views of those who disagree with him?

ANDERSON, "STRUGGLING ALONE"

In this essay, Anderson recounts the experience of "Chris," a homosexual friend who kept his sexual orientation a secret from his family and most of his friends because he felt it was at odds with his religious beliefs. Anderson points out how even though Chris's university provides resources to support students confronting their sexual identity, Chris felt alienated by the group because of his religious beliefs about homosexuality. According to Anderson, this situation—where Chris must keep his orientation a secret from his religious community and his religious feelings about homosexuality a secret from the university community—suggests a problem with the way our culture treats homosexuality.

1. What is Anderson's argument? What evidence supports that argument?
2. "Chris" is depicted by Anderson as being very conflicted between his own expectations and desires and those of the cultural and social institutions to which he belongs. What are those institutions, and how do they create these conflicts within Chris? What sort of institution would help Chris achieve his desires without conflict?

3. Anderson chronicles how his relationship with Chris first made him angry, then sad, then inspired him. How does this reaction relate to Chris's dilemma? Is it beneficial or hurtful?

ISSUE IN FOCUS: SAME-SEX MARRIAGE

This "Issue in Focus" section contains several essays about the hotly debated topic of same-sex marriage. While some actively pursue same-sex marriage as a civil rights issue, others find it a good step for pragmatic social reasons. On the other side, some politicians have proposed legislation that would constitutionally define marriage as between one man and one woman. Many of the arguments against same-sex marriage invoke the idea of "natural law" (homosexuality isn't natural) in some form. This section begins with some introductory material, including a carton by Matt Davies about the political battles over same-sex marriage, as well as the text of a 1996 version of a Defense of Marriage Act, the latter of which is included to give an example of a proposal with major ramifications. This section can be useful for thinking about what aspects of society would change if the proposal were to be accepted. It also can serve as an introduction to the language, style, and tone of congressional documents.

The next three short essays take varying positions on same-sex marriage. Quindlen's article, "Evan's Two Moms," which appeared in the *New York Times* in 1992, makes many kinds of claims—definitions, evaluations, proposals—but at heart, her argument is definitional. The "linchpin of family," she writes, "has commonly been a loving commitment between two adults." Students may not be familiar with the "op-ed piece" as a genre. You might bring a copy of the *New York Times* to class and show students where brief pieces such as this one appear in the paper. What expectations do readers have when they read such articles? Has Quindlen met or thwarted those expectations?

DAVIES, "WE'RE HERE TO DEFEND…" (CARTOON)

In this satirical cartoon, Puritans with pitchforks and torches prepare to assault the Constitution, which is defended by a lonely court system, in the name of an "Anti-Gay Marriage Amendment."

1. What is Davies's argument? What evidence is used to support that argument?
2. What extra meaning does the dress of the characters in this cartoon lend to an interpretation of it?
3. What political position or positions does this cartoon support? What positions does it oppose? What elements of the cartoon suggest these connections?

THE DEFENSE OF MARRIAGE ACT

This act, which was signed into law by President Clinton in 1996, had two purposes: 1) to make sure that no state had to recognize same-sex marriages in another state and 2) to define "marriage" and the term "spouse" in such a way so that the federal government would only recognize traditional, mixed-gender marriages.

1. What unique features do you find in the congressional proposal? How does it differ in style from other articles included here? What elements of its context and special role (as a potential law or amendment) impact the language used by its authors?
2. Are the definitions of "marriage" and "spouse" as explicitly stated in the act different from the implicit definitions of these two terms as used by Quindlen and Geis? Are they the same?
3. What are the differences in motivation and effect between the two stated goals of the act? In other words, is the first goal—to make sure that no state forces its definition of "marriage" on any other state—as objectionable to pro-same-sex marriage activists as the second goal—to define "marriage" as a union between a man and a woman? Why or why not?

QUINDLEN, "EVAN'S TWO MOMS"

This article was published in the *New York Times* in 1992. In it, Quindlen describes the plight of Evan, who had to be adopted by his biological mother's lesbian lover in order to have her legally recognized as his guardian. Quindlen uses this example and others like it to question what constitutes a family and what legal protections should be offered to non-traditional families like Evan's.

1. What is Quindlen's argument, and what evidence does she use to support that argument?
2. According to Quindlen, how do the attitudes of gay people and straight people differ regarding gay marriage?
3. Consider Quindlen's argumentative strategy. If her argument is at heart definitional, why does she wait until the fifth paragraph to define "family" in specific terms? Do the fragments at the end of the first paragraph forecast her argument? If so, how? And is the style in which they are written significant? You may stress to your students that questions such as these don't have single correct answers. Rather, the questions are designed to help students develop their own claims about the relationship between Quindlen's claims and central purpose and the decisions she made in shaping her text.
4. Examine how Quindlen uses references to the civil rights movement as an argumentative tool. Why choose this particular historical example? What does Quindlen hope to achieve by making this comparison?

GEIS, "A NEW TACTIC IN FIGHTING MARRIAGE INITIATIVES"

This article examines some of the fallout of marriage initiatives designed to prevent the recognition of homosexual marriage: according to Geis, out of "28 state marriage initiatives, 17 have included language outlawing domestic partnerships" as well. That is, these initiatives often affect straight couples, a fact which Geis notes is being used to rally heterosexual citizens against marriage initiatives.

1. What is Geis's argument, and what evidence does she use to support that argument?

2. Consider the opening paragraphs of Geis's essay. How does her use of this introduction affect the response to her argument? What audience does she seem to tailoring this argument to?
3. How does characterizing the debate over marriage initiatives using political affiliations ("libertarian") or non-homosexual unions affect the question of homosexual civil rights?

JASPER, "SUBVERSION THROUGH PERVERSION"

Jasper begins his essay by trying to connect with his audience on the assumption that television in general is a pretty bad thing. He also assumes that his audience considers homosexuality to be a negative or dangerous thing. Jasper argues that there is an active campaign to normalize and give positive images of homosexuality in the media. He considers this an attack on many traditional American values. Jasper uses quotes from members of the entertainment industry and uses examples from televisions shows (such as "The O.C." and "The Simpsons") to establish this "subversive" campaign.

Jasper uses the strong language of "revolution" to describe the increasing focus on homosexuality in popular media. He argues that this "propaganda campaign" can ruin America, and again assumes that it must be stopped.

1. What assumptions does Jasper make about his audience? What does he seem to expect them to do or think differently after reading his article? Discuss the context in which the article first appeared (see the introduction to it).
2. What emotionally loaded terms does Jasper use? How do terms like "revolution," "propaganda," and "mafia" connect to other cultural events or historical moments? What do they make you think of?
3. What role does the "Simpsons" reference play in the context of this article? For what kind of audience or audiences would this reference improve the reception of Jasper's argument? Harm it?
4. What is the "Velvet Mafia" in Jasper's article? How is this term a type of pathos argument? Is it also a logical fallacy of sorts?
5. Jasper considers the television media to be a very powerful cultural

force. Do you agree with this? In what ways does television media shape your values or the values of those around you?

HAERINGER, "COMING OUT IN THE LINE OF FIRE"

The wars in Afghanistan and Iraq have tested the limits of the U.S. military and slowed military recruiting—facts which have made retaining seasoned soldiers an important goal of the armed forces. In this article, Haeringer investigates the fallout of the military's long-standing ban on homosexuals, known as the "don't ask, don't tell" policy, on homosexual servicemen and women.

1. What is Haeringer's primary claim? What evidence does he use to support that claim?
2. The U.S. military command argues that allowing openly homosexual personnel in the military would undermine its effectiveness. What evidence is given to support this claim? Do you find it persuasive? Does Haeringer attempt to rebut it? If so, how does he do this, and is he successful?
3. How does Haeringer's use of terms like "valor" affect the reception of his argument?
4. What do you think of Haeringer's argument that the military's "Don't Ask, Don't Tell" policy forces the military to turn loyal soldiers into "bad guy[s]"?

MARTIN AND SCHWARTZMANN, "BAD FOR BOTH BOYS AND GIRLS"

This short essay takes on the policy of sex-segregated education, arguing that the scientific discoveries that back these plans are merely "dressed up versions of old stereotypes" about male and female behavior.

1. What is the argument of this essay? What evidence is provided to support that argument?
2. According to Martin and Schwartzmann, what are the arguments for sex-segregated schooling. Are these arguments presented fairly—in

other words, would Martin and Schwartzmann's opponents recognize these arguments as their own? Do Martin and Schwartzmann successfully rebut these arguments?

3. In this short article, the authors have very little room to present detailed evidence to support their rebuttal. Without this option, how are their claims defended? Do they primarily use ethos, pathos, or logos? For which audiences are their techniques likely to be effective?

SULLIVAN, "THE END OF GAY CULTURE"

In this long essay, Sullivan describes how distinctive gay culture is being destroyed by the mainstream acceptance of homosexuals. It is somewhat elegiac in tone, noting that the cultural acceptance that gay and lesbian activists have long worked for has helped to destroy a unique part of gay life.

1. What is Sullivan's argument? What evidence does he supply to support that argument?

2. What are the benefits of a distinctive gay culture listed by Sullivan? How is the disappearance of this distinctive culture similar to the disappearance of other minority cultures?

3. Are "tolerance" and "integration" as harmful to distinct cultures as Sullivan claims? If so, how are distinct cultures supposed to interact with each other?

4. Sullivan's essay is one of the longest in this collection. Using this extra space, is Sullivan able to make more complex arguments? Does he provide more detailed evidence of his claims?

HACKBARTH "VANITY, THY NAME IS METROSEXUAL"

Alexa Hackbarth's article is more lighthearted than some of the others in this chapter. She focuses on the term "metrosexual," which has a variety of meanings, but which she defines as a "straight man who styles his hair using three different products, loves clothes and the very act of shopping for them, and describes himself as sensitive and romantic."

She goes on to talk about her own dating experiences in the Washington, D.C. area. She complains that the men she dates all seem to be metrosexual, and she isn't sure she likes that. The article turns a bit more cynical when Hackbarth wonders if this tendency towards metrosexuality is a "result of marketing and advertising pressure." Here, Hackbarth focuses on the role of media as well, in terms of its power to create images of masculinity, of what is desirable, and of what is acceptable. Hackbarth shows concern that metrosexuality is simply another version of consumerism and that it fills in for something more meaningful, something missing in people's lives. She leaves that missing thing to the imagination.

The term "metrosexual" is one that many in your class will be familiar with, and some might even be willing to self-identify that way. They may be able to provide definitions of "metrosexual" from their own experiences.

1. How does your students' definition of "metrosexual" differ from Hackbarth's? What kinds of definitions does she use (metaphorical, categorical, descriptive, what it is not, other)?
2. What is the power and role of the media (in terms of sexual identity, for example) according to Hackbarth? How does this role of the media compare with Jasper's argument? Are there ways that they agree significantly about the power of popular media, even if they do not agree about issues of sexuality?
3. What role does Hackbarth's stories of her dating life play in this article? How do they add or detract from the points she is trying to make? Be sure to take the context of where the article appeared (*Washington Post*) and the audience into account.
4. What cause and effect relationships does Hackbarth suggest in the latter half of her article? How does she rhetorically try to draw those connections?

IN-CLASS ACTIVITIES

• Gomes's essay is organized in such a way that he first states his opponents' position, then makes new arguments based on the evidence his opponents use. Gomes shows how the scriptural interpretations used by fundamentalists are inaccurate. Ask students to find another argument based on the interpretation of evidence and refute that argument by reinterpreting the evidence.

• Gomes argues that the Bible does not make a priority of condemning homosexuality, but he does not deny that the Bible is not in favor of it. Is he finessing the distinction here and arguing based on his own prejudice? Have students rebut Gomes' arguments on his own terms, using the Bible verses that Gomes quotes.

• Like many of Quindlen's articles, "Homophobic? Read Your Bible" was published as an op-ed piece in the *New York Times*. Explain how Gomes would have to revise and expand this article if he were to publish it as an academic article, or as a feature essay in *Harper's*.

• Gather nine or ten of Quindlen's op-ed pieces from the *New York Times*. Have your students read these articles, then, in small groups, have them write a short description of Quindlen's characteristic rhetorical style. Describe her persona. Does she generally rely on logical, ethical, or pathetic appeals? Is she generally "liberal" or "conservative," or are those labels not particularly useful in describing her political convictions?

• Have your students gather examples of popular media—television, magazines, Web sites, movies—that they believe are designed to shape consumers' values. Have them briefly present this media with a short description of its possible influence, then discuss those influences as a class. Do the examples and subsequent discussions support Jasper's view of media influence?

SHORT ASSIGNMENTS

• Jasper argues that homosexuality is a definite wrong. Carmen Vazquez and many of the other writers in this unit would certainly disagree. And although Jasper, presumably, would never advocate violence against gay people, many gay activists and others accuse him and people who think like him of being indirectly responsible for gay bashing. Is this a valid claim? Write a causal argument asserting that claims like Jaspers are or are not responsible for gay-bashing.

• As with Gomes's article, political controversies often center on questions of "hermeneutics," or how to properly interpret written texts. An especially important example of a hermeneutic process is a Supreme Court decision, and the process of choosing and confirming Supreme Court justices often centers on how well that potential justice conforms to the Administration's and Congress' idea of how one should interpret the Constitution. Write a paper comparing Gomes' method of interpreting the Bible with the method of interpreting the Constitution advocated by the "strict constructionist" or "judicial activist" schools of interpretation.

• Like the military, most professional sports operate under unofficial "Don't Ask, Don't Tell" policies where athletes are discouraged from coming out as homosexuals. In a 1–2 page paper, have your students apply Haeringer's arguments against the military's enforced closeting of homosexuals to the implicit pressure on homosexual athletes to stay in the closet.

• What other reasons are there for the government to sanction gay marriage and domestic partnerships? Have students write a proposal argument that could be a companion piece to Quindlen's argument, but have them aim this argument at gay people who oppose gay marriage (they can do research on this position or use Quindlen's characterization of it).

• Have your students, individually or in small groups, select of a cultural value they would like to change (à la Hackbarth or Jasper). Then, have them design a media marketing campaign that would attempt to change cultural understandings of that issue and present it to the class. Finally, have them write a short analysis of why you made the rhetorical choices that you did.

• If we assume that metrosexuality is a useful term to describe a cultural change, we can think about what brought about that change. Responding to Hackbarth's conclusion about causes, write your own causal analysis of what leads to taking the role of a "metrosexual."

• Have your students research images of metrosexuals online. Then, have them choose an image and write a short visual analysis of it, informed by Hackbarth's essay.

Chapter 24: Globalization: Importing and Exporting America

As this collection of readings makes clear, debates over America's role in the world changed significantly after the terrorist attacks of September 11, 2001. Recent discussions of immigration make it clear that the terms of the debate have shifted. Along with immigration issues, the role of American culture in the world is under debate. Are American cultural objects and images something that hurt other societies? Are they simply desirable things that others can choose to take or reject as they wish? How do other cultures alter American icons and influence culture in the United States?

Moving to a new city to begin college involves many of the same experiences as moving to a new country and having moments of cultural mixing. As one assimilates, one gains insight not only into a new culture but also into the one left behind. In a small way, the experiences some of your students are having can be used as an analogy for some of the issues in these articles. Be sure to point out the differences as well, since the experience of immigrating is often a much more drastic change than going away to college.

PAYNE, "THE BAD NEWS IS..." (CARTOON)

Henry Payne's cartoon depicts Osama bin Laden checking his mail as he hides in a cave somewhere. It points out a possible contradiction in U.S. policies as a letter he receives notes, "The bad news is Operation Anaconda devastated our forces. The good news is the American INS approved your visa." When considering this cartoon, pay attention to the way the characters are visually portrayed. Items like the mailbox seem out of place and provide a sort of cultural mixing, while perhaps creating a humorous contradiction with bin Laden's cave.

1. How would you describe the characters in this cartoon? What stereo-types are used and/or broken in the way they are drawn?
2. What is Payne saying about U.S. immigration policy with this cartoon? Who are the various possible targets of Payne's critique?
3. How would this cartoon change if the caption was different or if there was no caption? Discuss the role of captions in directing how one "reads" or views different images.

NGAI, "NO HUMAN BEING IS ILLEGAL"

Ngai's essay discusses the discourse of the immigration debate, noting the pitfalls of generalizing or making sweeping statements about immigrants. She argues that terms like "illegal immigrant" are used to bolster U.S. nationalism and sovereignty and that they create uncomfortable connections between immigrants and the "war on terror."

1. What is Ngai's argument, and how does she support that argument with evidence?
2. What are some reasons why Ngai would begin her essay with refer-ences to abortion, gun control, and the division in the Republican party over immigration?
3. If you were not aware that Ngai's article originally appeared in a quarterly journal, what evidence from its style or tone would indicate this fact? How do these distinct features affect the reception of Ngai's argument?
4. How does Ngai's recontextualization of immigration arguments to include non-Mexican immigrants affect the reception of her argu-ment?

LAZARUS, "THE NEW COLOSSUS"

This short poem mythologizes the Statue of Liberty; some of its lines have become well known as a motto for U.S. openness to immigrants.

1. What is the argument of Lazarus's poem? How is that argument sup-ported?
2. What is a "Colossus"? How does this image affect the meaning of the poem?

3. How does the placement of Lazarus's poem within Ngai's essay change the way you and your students understand its famous lines?
4. What does Lazarus's use of phrases like "huddled masses" and "wretched refuse" imply about immigrants. Why does Lazarus use this language? Does the idea represented in lines 10–14 still seem representative of U.S. immigration policy?

ALDRICH, "THE UNGUARDED GATES"

Similar to Lazarus's poem, this piece uses the heightened language of poetry to mythologize the United States' historic openness to immigration. However, unlike Lazarus, Aldrich warns against letting just anyone in to the country, for doing so could "waste the fight of freedom."

1. What is the argument of Aldrich's poem? How does he support that argument?
2. Compare the argument of Aldrich's poem to that of Lazarus's poem. How are they different? What similarities do the two works have?

MALKIN, "BEWARE OF ILLEGAL ALIENS SEEKING HAZMAT LICENSES"

In this article, pundit Michelle Malkin describes how allowing illegal immigrants to get driver's licenses could open up the country to terrorists using these forms of identification to move freely about the country.

1. What is Malkin's argument? What evidence does she use to support it?
2. In paragraph 3 of this essay, Malkin quotes a police official describing Mullawala's "suspicious behavior." How convincing do you find this evidence and the comparison that Malkin makes between it and the events of September 11, 2001?
3. How does Malkin make the connection between her opposition to driver's licenses for illegal immigrants and terrorist use of those licenses?

EPSTEIN, "IMMIGRATION MAZE"

In this article, Helen Epstein exposes a problem with U.S. immigration policies that is rarely remarked on in the immigration debate: legal immigration. She describes the difficulties that she and her husband faced trying to process his legal immigration to the United States.

1. What is Epstein's argument, and what evidence does she use to support it?
2. How does Epstein suggest the U.S. should balance the problem of delays in immigration bureaucracy and the problem of national security?
3. Is Epstein able to transform her personal experience with immigration bureaucracy into an issue that is relevant to a wider group of people? If so, how?

MILLER, "WHAT'S THE WORST THAT CAN HAPPEN . . . ?"

In this cartoon, Wiley Miller highlights the irony in the immigration debate, noting that most Americans either immigrated to this country or are descended from immigrants.

1. What is Miller's argument? How is that argument supported?
2. What is the irony of the situation depicted here? How does it apply to the current discussion of immigration?
3. Compare the argument of this cartoon with that of the two poems in this chapter. How are they the same? How are they different?

GITLIN, "UNDER THE SIGN OF MICKEY MOUSE AND CO."

Todd Gitlin argues that "media flow defies national boundaries." He reflects on the power of media to cross borders, but wants his audience to remember that the people who receive these messages are often in very different economic situations. Gitlin claims that the United States is the center or main originator of this media flow. He uses examples of American-based movies, brands, celebrities, and images that are extremely popular in a variety of different countries to suggest that the closest thing to a "common cultural zone" in the world is American popular culture.

Gitlin reminds us that this flow of media is not just one-way. Images are altered and mixed with ideas from new sources before they flow back into American culture. While this state of affairs can be taken as a form of American imperialism, Gitlin reminds his readers that many products and images are wanted and liked. The essay focuses on consumption and entertainment, and the ease with which one can consume different media transfers over to a flexibility in identity. Gitlin says that people expect to be entertained and to go with the flow of images until they find goods they connect with for a while.

You may have to explain what Gitlin is referring to when he talks about "modernity" in this essay. Your students will probably have many examples of unique mixes of media, and can probably add to Gitlin's list of internationally popular aspects of the American culture industry. Gitlin seems more interested in having his audience pay attention to these cultural flows than in saying they are necessarily good or bad. That critique can be left for the students to discuss.

1. Which of the cultural artifacts Gitlin discusses are you familiar with? Which do you not know about? What cultural exports from outside the United States do you like or connect with?
2. Does Gitlin have a clear argument here? Is he trying to say that this American cultural dominance is good or bad in some way? What does he assume his audience will think?
3. What is "identity" or how does one create an "identity" according to Gitlin? What contrasting notions of identity can you think of?
4. Gitlin lists numerous celebrities, brands, movies, etc. How do these impact his ethos? How would his ethos be different (perhaps work for a different audience) if he had chosen different examples (maybe more rap artists, independent films, or reality television shows)?
5. How is "culture" defined in this essay? If it does not seem clearly defined, what can you gather from the essay as a whole? How might you alter that definition?

BUTALIA, "LIVING THE DREAM"

In this article, Butalia describes the development of women's liberty in India. She does this primarily by relating the stories of young women in India who are able, at least in some small way, to take control of their lives.

1. What is Butalia's argument? What evidence is used to support that argument?
2. What is the 'dream' in Butalia's title? Does she use this word satirically or sincerely (or both)?
3. Can Butalia's description of Indian culture be applied to U.S. culture? If so, how should readers from the U.S. respond to her essay?

CARLSEN, "WAL-MART VS. PYRAMIDS"

Laura Carlsen's article has a more journalistic style than many of the others, but it still is argumentative. She chooses particular pieces of information to give in a fairly objective tone, and defines the "real issue" in such a way as to argue that Wal-Mart is wrong in building a new store near the Pyramid of the Sun from the Teotihuacan Empire.

Carlsen initially provides details about Wal-Mart's building plans while using phrases like "commercial conquest" to connect Wal-Mart to notions of imperialism. She uses the Teotihuacan Empire as a foil for the Wal-Mart "Empire" in giving a short history of Wal-Mart's growth and labor practices. Carlsen then reflects on the resistance to the new Wal-Mart store and claims the "battle" is a "struggle over a country's right to define itself."

Wal-Mart is often both popular and controversial in the United States of America. Some students will already know the advantages and disadvantages of a Wal-Mart. The language Carlsen uses and her journalistic style can be important issues to discuss as part of her argumentative strategies.

1. Identify the different references to battle, war, or struggle in the article. What tone do these terms create and what do they suggest that the author wants to argue?

2. How might this article change if it were written to Wal-Mart employees?
3. Carlsen gives a couple of short history lessons in this article. How do they serve as logos, ethos, and/or pathos arguments?
4. What do you think of this article as a type of journalism? How is it "objective" or not? In what contexts is it appropriate and where might it not be appropriate in this journalistic format?

DEARDORFF, FROM *IN SEARCH OF INTERCULTURAL COMPETENCE*

In this essay, Deardorff argues that developing the "intercultural competence" of students in higher education is an important goal for U.S. universities. However, it is not clear how this competence will be achieved. She proposes a means for measuring intercultural competence and outlines the benefits that will result from achieving this competence.

1. What is Deardorff's argument? What evidence does she provide to support it?
2. According to Deardorff, what is "intercultural competence"? How does Deardorff respond to the use of statistics in its definition?
3. Identify logos, ethos, and pathos arguments in the essay. How are they integrated and made to work together (or not)?
4. What kind of argument is this essay (proposal, definition, causal, etc.)? Does it combine arguments in some way? How are these multiple arguments put together?

IN-CLASS ACTIVITIES

• Individually or in small groups, have your students create their own political cartoon about some aspect of America's role in the larger world.

• Divide your students into small groups, and assign each group one of the cartoons or photographs featured in this chapter. Then have each group write three or four alternate captions for the image they have been assigned. Have the groups present their alternate captions, and discuss how the new text affects the impact of the images.

• Repeat the exercise above, except, instead of composing new captions, have your students write a short visual analysis of the images in this chapter.

• Have your students create a list of cultural items that best fit their identity, or, instead, create a list that represents what they think of as "American culture." Provide some analysis of why they chose the items they did.

• Have your students take the role of a high-level Wal-Mart administrator and write a press release about the new store described in the Carlsen essay.

• Get your students to collect images of American culture from magazines or other sources. Have them present the images to the class, using an example from a text in this chapter to illustrate how the image typifies that culture.

SHORT ASSIGNMENTS

• In her essay, Ngai suggests that American immigration policy has led to an increase in "migrant exploitation." Have your students compose a short (1–2 page) paper exploring this connection. Specifically, have them explore the questions: Does the U.S. dependence on immigrant labor make it reluctant to speak out against immigrant abuse in other countries? How would stricter enforcement of illegal immigration statutes affect migrants' human rights?

• Have your students find an argument about the role of immigration issues in terrorism. Then, have them write a 1–2 page paper comparing that argument with one of the arguments presented in this chapter.

• Using Carlsen's article for some of your evidence, write a letter to Wal-Mart to convince them to change the location of this new store. Remember that you have to keep Wal-Mart owners' interests in mind.

• Have your students collect an image of recent Americana and then write a short visual analysis of that image.

Chapter 25: Science and Ethics

New technologies constantly introduce unique ethical dilemmas into scientific debates, ones that must be considered by scientists, politicians, and the general citizenry. Many of these issues are tied to questions of biology and what it means to be human. Advances in cloning, for example, have prompted many to try to define what a "real" human is. Questions about the ethical use of technology have very practical consequences regarding safety and the possible abuse of technology.

For example, nanotechnology is the science of molecule-sized organisms and machines. This technology is already in use in some microchips, rocket fuel, and makeup. Many hope that nanotechnology can help us make machines so small they can enter the human bloodstream and repair cells or do other medical work. However, this use begs the question: if these machines can do so much and are extremely difficult to locate due to their size, what risks will they create?

Nanotechnology is just one emerging technology discussed in the following essays. This chapter also includes articles which focus on cloning, human and otherwise; robots; stem-cell research; and the role of science in society. In each case, you will find that if you strive to connect these issues to news articles or controversies that are ongoing and quite public, it will help to spark more engaged responses from your students.

JOY, "WHY THE FUTURE DOESN'T NEED US"

Bill Joy is a major figure in the world of computer technologies, so many would assume that he would be in favor of pushing for nanotechnology research (among other technologies). However, he describes major ethical concerns that come from his work in developing new technologies that caused many to step back a bit. His position as a cofounder of Sun Microsystems and the creator of computer languages made his cautionary voice one that was heard well.

Joy talks about his concern with new technologies by telling the story about meeting with Ray Kurzweil (an inventor and computer science professor) in which Joy reads part of Kurzweil's utopian book about humans changing as they merge with new technologies. However, Joy finds the dystopian elements most compelling and worrisome. He quotes a long passage from this book, *The Age of Spiritual Machines*, and then goes on to discuss and quote from a more directly dystopian book by Hans Moravec. Joy provides a narrative of his thinking process by giving glimpses of conversations he had, places he traveled, and books he read, all in order to show his transformation—even conversion—to a more cautionary position. He allows the reader to join with him on this process, perhaps in hopes that the reader can undergo a similar sort of transformation without quite so much time and work.

Joy refers to numerous science fiction books and shows, pointing out how they are not so futuristic any more. He notes that many technologies promise some form of near-immortality, and that this is where those technologies may become most dangerous. For instance, in the case of nanotechnology he claims the technology "can spawn whole new classes of accidents and abuses," especially because it can be used by individuals. Joy jumps back to the history of his growing up years and his own work on computer technologies—continuing to build his ethos—and then reflects on his unease that his own work may help build creatures that eventually replace humans.

While Joy writes with a calm, reflective tone, he provides some doomsday scenarios. The extremity of the positive and negative possibilities Joy displays are something for your class to consider, as they may find this article to be science fiction of a sort as well. You may need to introduce some of the technologies Joy discusses, or find someone in your class who knows about them. This is also a good article to read together with science fiction material that projects current worries onto future technologies.

1. Who is Joy's target audience in this article? What do you know about *Wired* magazine, where the article appears?
2. How does Joy use ethos arguments in this article? Why did this article shock many people when it came out?

3. Joy describes his own thought process and experience of change. Why does he use this rhetorical tactic? What does he seem to hope the audience will do as they read along?

4. Joy gives many projections of the future—both his own and from other people. What evidence does he give for some of these projections? What makes one or several more compelling than others?

5. What ethical questions does Joy raise? What does he want his audience to be asking? How would you describe Joy's ethics?

FUKUYAMA, "TALE OF TWO DYSTOPIAS"

Francis Fukuyama argues that there are many different ways to regulate technology. Even though some say that technology's advance cannot be slowed, he says that regulations must be thoughtfully made. Particularly with various forms of biotechnology we need to think about the practical and ethical ramifications of different advances.

Fukuyama begins this excerpt from his book *Our Posthuman Future* with references to two famous stories about frightening future societies: George Orwell's *1984* and Aldous Huxley's *Brave New World*. He says that the subtle form of control in Huxley's book is both more dangerous and more compelling than that depicted by Orwell; essentially, he claims that we have to be aware of the dangers in getting everything we want. The possibilities of control and change that new biotechnologies give, according to Fukuyama, are such that they risk changing what it means to be human. He says we have to ask if changing what it means to be human is a bad thing, and in the end, he argues that it is. He gives three scenarios as examples of how the end of humans as we know them could be horrifying.

Fukuyama wants to use the state to regulate technologies. He says this is practical, and while not perfect, has been effective in the past. Several issues are in the debate here. A class might discuss the kinds of literary and doomsday-scenario evidence Fukuyama uses, they might discuss the level of risk that these technologies actually pose, and they might discuss the proposed solution of using state regulation to keep things fairly safe.

1. What does it mean to be human according to Fukuyama? Is this idea of "humanity" a flexible one (according to him or you)?

2. Talk about how Fukuyama's examples and scary scenarios work as arguments. What kinds of arguments are they and to whom do they appeal?
3. What are the other positions on biotechnology that Fukuyama seems to be presenting and even arguing against?
4. Compare the styles that Fukuyama and Joy use in presenting their warnings.

MERKLE, "NANOTECHNOLOGY: DESIGNS FOR THE FUTURE"

Ralph Merkle engages in a conversation with a writer for *Ubiquity*, a Web-based publication of the Association for Computing Machinery. In many ways, Merkle responds directly to Bill Joy's argument printed just a few pages earlier. Much of the interview covers Merkle's work and a nanotechnology group called The Foresight Institute. However, he also argues that while nanotechnology may have its dangers, they should not prevent research in the field. The goal is to use nanotechnology for good purposes, allowing for ethical debate, but continuing to work on a technology allows for greater understanding of it, including its dangers. Merkle goes on to list a number of major areas that nanotechnology could help with, including poverty and medical issues. He focuses on these basic human needs, and even suggests that nanotechnology could help economic growth and equality.

Merkle is optimistic about nanotechnology, and speculates about some pretty impressive changes that may make many people skeptical. He does give some detail in his examples, but one issue to consider with the class is the vast difference between his projections and Joy's projections. Consider how each one makes a case for what the future could be like.

1. What is the setting for this interview? How does the interview set-up change the rhetorical situation in comparison to an essay like Joy's or Fukuyama's?
2. What evidence does Merkle give to support his claims about the benefits of nanotechnology?
3. What basic points do Merkle and Joy agree on? How does Merkle respond to Joy (consider tone, argument types, style)?

4. What is "relinquishment"? Why doesn't Merkle like it? Is that what Joy was arguing for?

FRANKLIN, "BEAUTIFUL, FUNCTIONAL, AND FRUGAL"

1. What is Franklin's argument, and how does she support these arguments?
2. Have your students identify the features of this talk that indicate its origins as an oral text.
3. Discuss with your students Franklin's argument that science, via its study of nature, can provide a model for the structure of society. Should scientists be involved in political issues like this one?
4. What is the occasion of Franklin's speech? How does it affect your reading of her text?

GATES, "A ROBOT IN EVERY HOME"

Bill Gates, the co-founder of software giant Microsoft, suggests in this essay that the next great development in personal technology will be the introduction of robots into individual homes. He then outlines the developments in robotics that could make this possible, and the ways that personal robots could help improve people's lives.

1. What is Gates's argument? What evidence does he use to support it?
2. Is Gates's comparison between the development of computers and robotics a valid one?
3. Gates's essay covers some very technical topics. Is it readable when the reader doesn't understand all of the technologies being discussed? If so, how does Gates accomplish this?

SOARES, "ATTITUDE SCREEN"

Christine Soares introduces developments in gene research that will make it possible to screen for genetic dispositions to certain illnesses. She then discusses the effect that these screenings might have on individuals and the moral and ethical questions raised by this technology.

1. What is Soares's argument, and what evidence does she use to support that argument?

2. Compare Soares's argument about DNA databases and genetic screening with some of the other arguments about future technologies included in this chapter. Even if it is desirable to avoid genetic screening, is it possible to prevent the deployment of this technology?

3. Is genetic testing a completely scientific issue? What are the ethical and moral implications of the practice?

ISSUE IN FOCUS: STEM CELL RESEARCH

This section of the chapter focuses directly on stem cell research, particularly on scientific, ethical, and political debates about "research" or "therapeutic" cloning to create new stem cells to harvest. This debate has gained prominence through the endorsement of a number of celebrities, from the late Christopher Reeve to Nancy Reagan. People can approach the debate from so many different starting points in terms of values that finding the real point of disagreement can be difficult and emotionally charged.

This section provides just a few voices in the public debate over stem cell research, starting with Ron Reagan's speech at the 2004 Democratic National Convention. The speech caused some controversy since Ron Reagan is the son of former President Ronald Reagan. Ron Reagan focuses on the benefits for medical conditions that stem cell research can have, and uses the example of a 13-year-old with diabetes in his speech.

Steven Milloy responds directly to Reagan's speech, calling his argument "junk-science." Milloy asserts that stem cell research drains research funds while providing no real cures. Richard Doerflinger also responds to Reagan, asserting that the real agenda is human cloning, not medical help from stem cells. The "brave new world" shows up again in his article. This debate is all at one particular time, but you can find many other articles on stem cell research, and the cartoon at the beginning of the section also enters the debate by visually representing some of Ron Reagan's argument.

In this speech, Ron Reagan argues for increased government funding for stem cell research. According to Reagan, this research could help provide new therapies, and possibly even cures, for diseases like diabetes and Parkinson's.

1. What is Reagan's argument? What evidence does he provide to support it?
2. Is Reagan's essay a proposal? Why or why not?
3. How does Reagan deal with the possible ethos issues of presenting at the Democratic National Convention? How does he handle the difficult task of explaining a complicated technical procedure to a non-technical audience?
4. How does the celebrity status of many people talking about stem cells impact the debate (compared to a scientist, for example)? How does that change the rhetorical situation? Can you think of a particular example of hearing about stem cell research from a celebrity figure?
5. Describe Reagan's example of the 13-year-old with diabetes in terms of pathos. Is it an effective appeal?

OLIPHANT, "THE RONALD REAGAN EULOGY WILL BE DELIVERED . . ."

In this comic, a tiny President Bush appears before a giant podium in what appears to be a cathedral where he will presumably deliver a eulogy for former President Ronald Reagan.

1. What is Oliphant's argument? How is that argument supported?
2. How is the composition and imagery of this comic "confrontational"?
3. What is the effect of the vast differences in size between the figure behind the podium and his surroundings?

MILLOY, "RON REAGAN WRONG ON STEM CELLS"

In this essay, Steven Milloy responds to Ron Reagan's call for increased funding for stem cell research, attacking Reagan's claims for the possibilities of this research.

1. What is Milloy's argument. What evidence does he use to rebut Reagan and support his own claims?
2. How effective is Milloy's essay as a rebuttal? Does it share the features of other types of arguments?
3. Milloy refers to Reagan's evidence as "junk-science." What does that term mean? What does it mean as a critique of Reagan?
4. It seems that political concerns—the preference for private funding of research over public funding—in some way motivate Milloy's argument. Does Reagan's argument exhibit similar political assumptions about the best role of government in research? If so, what are those assumptions?

DOERFLINGER, "DON'T CLONE RON REAGAN'S AGENDA"

Like Milloy, Doerflinger doesn't agree with Reagan's claims about stem cell research. While not as hostile to Reagan as Milloy, Doerflinger takes issue with the implication in Reagan's speech that increasing research into stem cell cures for Parkinson's and diabetes is tantamount to a call for increases in human cloning.

1. What is Doerflinger's argument, and what evidence does he provide to support it?
2. In paragraph two of the essay, Doerflinger claims that Reagan's speech advocates human cloning. Is this a fair characterization of Reagan's speech? Where in Reagan's text is this argument made?
3. At the end of the essay, Doerflinger connects cloning to the dystopia of *Brave New World*. What is the connection between this technology and the dystopia? Is the comparison apt?
4. Did the two rebuttals change your understanding of Ron Reagan's argument? If so, how? If not, why did they fail to do so?
5. These three short articles are ostensibly written in response to each

other in some way, but are delivered in different settings. How might those settings impact these articles?

6. What is the "real" issue with stem cell research according to each article? How does each defend that position?

IN-CLASS ACTIVITIES

• Compare Joy and Merkle's views of new technologies—particularly nanotechnology. What are their main points of agreement and disagreement? Divide your class in two and have one half debate Joy's point of view and the other Merkle's.

• What is the fundamental problem being dealt with in Fukuyama's essay? What other solutions, besides state regulation, can you think of? Have your students conduct a mock debate where they argue for the two sides.

• Think of a political or social group that might disagree with Merkle's optimism about science. Write a rebuttal from their perspective.

• Merkle projects quite a few cause-effect relationships. Identify several of these and then analyze one in terms of how he argues that a particular event will lead to a particular effect. What alternate results can you think of?

• When Bill Gates talks about there being a computer on every desk, he means every desk in the wealthy, industrialized world. What about technology in underprivileged countries? Have your students do some research on the effects of technology in the third world and present their results to the class.

• Divide your students into groups of 2–3 and have them choose an audience invested in the debate over stem cell research (researchers, doctors, the ill). Then, have them outline a political speech for that audience, either arguing for or against federal funding of stem cell research.

SHORT ASSIGNMENTS

• Have your students write a brief utopian or dystopian scenario involving a new technology.

• Have your students write a process story where they show how a change occurred in their thinking about a particular issue, and then use that story as part of an argument that attempts to persuade an audience.

• Direct your students to choose a particular aspect of contemporary biotechnology to research. Then have them write a proposal that suggests a way to legislate that technology to keep it safe as well as useful.

• Write a conversation between Merkle and Joy about nanotechnology based on these articles in this chapter and a few others you can find.

• Bill Gates's essay doesn't spend much time discussing the effect of having a robot in every home. Have your students research some possible uses for personal robots, and then write short proposals where they argue either for the benefits or the drawbacks of robot technology.

• Take the position of Ron Reagan and write a response to Milloy and Doerflinger.

• Have your students create collages of quotes and visuals relating to stem cell research. Encourage them to try to make a particular argument for one side of the debate or about the debate itself in their collages.

Chapter 26: Privacy

A variety of new technologies provide new challenges and debates about the preservation and definition of privacy. Cell phone cameras, online banking, and information about genetic risk factors are just three examples of advances in technology prompting a reexamination of privacy debates. For example, the popular Web site Facebook.com (which originally catered exclusively to college students) is designed for friends to connect, talk, and share information. However, it has also been used by law enforcement officers (for example) to help identify suspects and to locate possible guilty parties in vandalism incidents. Is this an invasion of privacy, or is the information entirely public?

BRIN, "THREE CHEERS FOR THE SURVEILLANCE SOCIETY!"

David Brin's title gives away that he is taking a more lighthearted approach to surveillance than the other authors in this chapter. Brin makes a serious argument however. He suggests that while new forms of surveillance will come and are serious issues, the real concern is that they be used not just by the government for observing the people, but also by the people for looking back at the government. As long as the surveillance is a two-way street, Brin thinks things will be okay. Privacy may change, but tyranny will come only when the observation is uni-directional.

Brin gives examples of coming technology that will track your preferences and needs in useful but sometimes disconcerting ways. He discusses chips that will easily be put into all sorts of objects for tracking, and simple cameras that will allow views from anywhere on earth. While these might seem frightening, they can create accountability by those in power as well, for they cannot escape the transparency of all this information either. Much of Brin's article consists of examples of new technologies that make surveillance easier. Most of them enhance human senses in some way or another (or enhance memory through databases). He argues that these new technologies will change what counts as private or personal data, and that the notion of privacy will have to change drastically. According to Brin, there is no "trade-off between security and freedom." We need and can have both, and they work together for Brin.

1. Which of the technologies Brin mentions seems the most useful? The most intrusive? Consider in detail the possible ramifications of that technology becoming widespread.
2. Brin lists many new technologies that can be useful surveillance tools. What are the effects of the accumulation of all these tools in his argument?
3. How does Brin use word choice and phrases to create an audience in his text? Describe the audience that his text seems to be addressing.
4. Is Brin's article a proposal? Why or why not?

KOPPEL, "TAKE MY PRIVACY, PLEASE!"

Ted Koppel is a familiar television figure, but here works in a written medium. He argues that while the Patriot Act may take some liberties, it is a small issue compared to new technologies that track people. One main example is OnStar, which tracks vehicles. He gives a sample conversation of how OnStar might help, but also provides warnings about the ease with which anyone can be tracked.

Koppel goes on to describe many other new technologies, not unlike Brin's listing of technologies. Koppel gives examples of instances where supposedly private information has been leaked, including from the Bank of America Corporation. He concludes by discussing legislation to protect privacy and to require notifying people whose information may have been leaked. However, he says much more needs to be done.

Koppel's article is another that gives many warnings and examples, but spends less time on any proposal. His news figure status may give his argument more or less weight for different students. One issue to continue addressing is the use of numerous technology examples—which may be compelling to various audiences, but have little in terms of evidence for what actually will happen with them.

1. Compare Koppel's technology list with others from this chapter (such as Brin's). How do the lists vary for different audiences and

arguments they are trying to make? Do the examples serve different functions in their arguments?

2. While different privacy issues are at stake? How might Brin, Koppel, and Larsen be in conversation with one another? What issues do they hold in common and on what issues do they differ?

3. Discuss how Koppel's tone in this article differs from his tone on television news shows. How does the context impact that tone?

MCPHERSON, "IT'S PART OF THE GOVERNMENT'S NEW EMPHASIS . . ."

This cartoon by John McPherson satirizes the Catch-22 of our technological society, where new products and services can often leave consumers vulnerable to troubles that they aren't even aware of having.

1. What is McPherson's argument? What evidence is used to support that argument?

2. What are the connotations that the image of the hooded shoppers carry? How does this context affect your reading of the comic?

LARSEN, "TRAVELER'S CARD MIGHT JUST PAVE THE WAY FOR A NATIONAL ID CARD"

Randall Larsen's short argument about ID cards suggests that creating a national ID card might now make us more secure than not having one. He sets up the issue as security against the intrusive collection of information, and worries how easy it is to travel under a false identity. He argues that a traveler's card would be a good step towards a national ID card.

Larsen mentions a senator who changed from being against to being in favor of national ID cards with biometric information. Larsen says that the change is because inaction is now seen as a greater risk than the action of creating the cards. Much of this ties in to terrorism fears. Larsen supports the cards by noting that 15 countries in Europe have them. He identifies four questions to be asked about creating ID cards, and says that the main hindrances right now are public opinion and ensuring that "ID credentials are properly issued." These are tough problems to solve, and he considers travelers' cards to be a good step until a national card can be created.

It might be difficult for students to initially understand the exigency of this issue. Larsen does not spend much time explaining how ID cards would help more than current identification cards. This article is useful for considering how much the fear of terrorism impacts national policies and debates.

1. What is the exigency of Larsen's argument? What does he worry about?
2. What sorts of evidence does Larsen use?
3. The introduction of National ID cards is probably an issue that you do not often think about, a fact which Larsen seems aware of. How does he attempt to get the audience invested enough in the issue to act, or at least, to think about it more?
4. How might Koppel and Larsen respond to each other's arguments? They are on somewhat different issues, but both have elements of tracking, security, privacy, and travel.
5. What feasibility issues are involved in Larsen's article? How do these feasibility issues lead him to suggesting travelers' cards?

BURK, "COUNSELORS WALK A FINE LINE WEIGHING RIGHTS OF STUDENT AND COLLEGE"

In her article, Burk points out the increasing call for colleges and universities to monitor the mental health treatment of their students. While it is hoped this monitoring will help prevent tragic incidents like the Virginia Tech shootings, Burk notes that tracking students with mental health issues is a very difficult task for most educational institutions.

1. What is Burk's argument? What evidence does she provide to support it?
2. At what point should colleges give up student privacy for safety?
3. Based on your reading of Burk's article, do you think colleges should have blanket policies towards possibly violent students, or should they deal with students individually, on a case by case basis?

ZASLOW, "THE END OF YOUTHFUL INDISCRETIONS: INTER-NET MAKES THEM PERMANENT BLOTS"

Jeffrey Zaslow argues that young people today need to be concerned about privacy rights related to information and opinions they put on the Internet. By the time they are applying for jobs and getting their own insurance, he argues, they are likely to have an extensive Web history and presence. Potential employers, for example, could easily access much of this information, and might use statements from years earlier as reasons not to hire someone. Web logs that confess one's random political thoughts, personal angers, or other potentially volatile information could be dangerous for a person's future according to Zaslow.

Zaslow yearns for a little more privacy as he notes how information online is so often incomplete and out of context. He suggests removing potentially problematic references to ourselves on the Internet, along with being aware of other forms of surveillance. He mostly wants further debate on the ethics of privacy in a Google-driven world.

1. How often do you Google people? Whom do you Google? Do you ever ask permission first? What ethical considerations might there be about Googling someone?
2. What sort of personal information have you put online? Are you concerned about that information? How do you feel about a potential employer looking you up online?
3. How does Zaslow's argument about privacy and the Internet differ from and work in comparison with Brin's argument?
4. What does Zaslow propose should be done about his Internet privacy concerns? Based on the other articles in this chapter, what other options can you think of? What general principles do (and should) these authors use concerning problems that require legislation about when government should not be involved?

ISSUE IN FOCUS: BIOMETRICS: MEASURING THE BODY FOR IDENTITY

It may be helpful to kick start your class's discussion of these readings by asking your students if they have ever been subjected to the kind of biometric scanning and collection described here. While most of your students will be familiar with some form of biometrics—picture IDs like driver's licenses and school IDs, for example—they may be less familiar with other forms of biometric identification. Beginning this discussion with familiar concerns should help ground your students' responses to the readings.

As with many of the other privacy concerns discussed in this chapter (and many of the issues considered in other chapters as well), most arguments related to using biometric information for identification can be discussed against the background of post-9/11 security concerns. As the title of this section clearly makes the connection between security and this biology-based form of data collection, your class's conversation about biometrics will likely be connected to the question of how much personal information are individuals willing to surrender in order to guarantee their personal safety.

BENNETT, "PRIVACY IMPLICATIONS OF BIOMETRICS"

Bennett describes biometrics—the tracking of identity using physical and biological features—and how biometrics is already a part of our culture in the form of fingerprinting and identification cards. He then explains how these readily accepted forms of biometrics are quite different from machine-assisted biometrics, noting the threat to privacy that this new development entails.

1. What is Bennett's argument? What evidence does he provide to support it?
2. How are machine biometrics different from more familiar biometrics like driver's licenses or fingerprints?
3. How have increases in computing technology made biometrics much more worrisome than before?
4. Can you or your students think of other examples of "data creep" that threaten privacy?

SAFFO, "A TRAIL OF DNA AND DATA"

Similar to Bennett, Saffo describes the future of biometric data collection, noting the potential of this technology to disturb contemporary understandings of privacy. He suggests that once biometric data is digitized, it runs the risk of being copied, creating the specter of biometric identity theft.

1. What is Saffo's argument? What evidence does he provide to support it?
2. Identify logos, pathos, and ethos elements in this article.
3. What are biometrics? How can one avoid those kinds of measures? Is it reasonable to even try to do so?
4. Saffo suggests that Americans talk as if they are interested in privacy but do not act that way. What do you think of this claim? What role does it play in his suggestion about what should be done for privacy? How does this claim impact his audience (which is one small segment of Americans)?

FBI, "USING TECHNOLOGY TO CATCH CRIMINALS"

This screenshot of an article on the FBI's Web site describes how the department uses fingerprinting to catch criminals at the border.

1. What is the argument of this Web page? What evidence is provided to support that argument?
2. How do the visual elements of this page affect its argument?

RYAN, "EMERGING BIOMETRIC TECHNOLOGIES" AND "VOICE VERIFICATION FOR TRANSACTIONS"

Ryan identifies several new biometric technologies used for identification, including dynamic signature analysis, keystroke dynamics, skin spectroscopy, vein patterning, body salinity, and facial thermography.

1. What is Ryan's argument? What evidence does he provide to support it?
2. Do Ryan and Bennett make different arguments? How does

Bennett's discussion of machine biometrics affect the biometric technologies described in this essay?

3. Why are biometrics needed to establish a person's identity? What is the importance of identity in our society?

4. What are some of the pitfalls that can be associated with using voice verification to identify a person over the phone?

5. Why are biometrics needed to establish a person's identity? What is the importance of identity in our society?

DOMKE, "WILL CASH AND CREDIT CARDS BECOME EXTINCT IN THE NOT-SO-DISTANT FUTURE?"

In this article, Domke suggests how biometric technology will be used in retail transactions. While some stores currently have RFID technology that doesn't require customers to swipe their credit cards, in the future these "contactless" means of payment could be replaced by payments made through cellphones or even chips embedded in customers' bodies.

1. What is Domke's argument? What evidence does he provide to support it?

2. What is dangerous about identity theft?

3. What benefits would there be to eliminating cash and credit cards?

4. How could biometric payment systems benefit non retail transactions? How could they help with identification of college students?

IN-CLASS ACTIVITIES

• Assume that you are hosting a serious television news show. You are interviewing Koppel on the topic of privacy. After reading this editorial, what questions might you ask? What might some of his responses be?

• Create an advertisement for TiVo. Then create a counter-ad that warns of its potential privacy dangers.

• Identify Koppel's thesis, main arguments for that thesis, and different pieces of evidence. Then choose one main rhetorical strategy he uses and describe it.

• Write a sample conversation where one person asks another for permission to Google him or her. Provide context for the conversation and a reflection on the ethical implications (or lack thereof) of this sort of request.

• Stage a classroom debate over biometrics. Divide your students into two groups, one which will argue for the use of biometric scanning, and one against it.

• Find a Web site or blog where people reveal a considerable amount of personal information. Write an essay analyzing the appearance of the site and the potential risks and benefits of presenting all this information online in that particular context.

• Compare Saffo and Koppel's articles. What differences and similarities do you find in their attitudes towards surveillance and privacy?

• What main values are implied by Saffo's article? What textual evidence supports your claims?

• As a class, perform a visual analysis of the FBI Web page.

SHORT ASSIGNMENTS

• Convert Brin's essay into a format more conducive to a Web site. Sketch what the pages of this Web site would be and select the information or sections that would go on each page. Also include what links between pages would be included. Feel free to edit his work significantly.

• What is Brin's main argument? How does he limit its scope? Compare his understanding of surveillance with one of the other readings from this chapter.

• Write a response informed by Saffo's article on biometrics that argues with Larsen's push for biometric national ID cards.

• Excerpt words and sentences from Larsen's article to make his argument as best you can in 150 words.

• Consider a proposed solution to a problem based on a few feasibility questions like the four Larsen asks.

130

Chapter 27: Regulating Substances, Regulating Bodies

Debates about the government regulation of substances are often about various drugs. However, all foods and drugs legally sold in the U.S. are regulated to some degree. Of course, most people think of illegal substances first. Marijuana is a common drug that has been made legal in California, for example, for medicinal purposes. Now smoking (cigarettes) is becoming more regulated in some places. Some cities have or are considering banning smoking in bars and restaurants.

Some drug regulation is based on the idea that a person using the drug may be a danger to others. However, regulation can more directly affect a person's body as well. With current concerns about weight and obesity in America, stricter fat content regulations or health regulations for foods are a debated issue. Various forms of plastic surgery have grown in popularity, and these are regulated as well. These different forms of regulation tie into the larger issue of what the government should and should not be involved in. When should an outside institution step in for the safety of a person or those around that person, and when should decisions be left to individuals? When should other strategies, such as education, be used instead of regulation?

CALIFANO, "THE RIGHT DRUG TO TARGET: CUTTING MARIJUANA USE"

Joseph Califano argues that not only is the U.S. government's focus on reducing marijuana use appropriate, but also that even greater efforts are needed. He argues that marijuana use should remain a crime, and that enforcing laws against its use reduces other crimes as well. Califano lists various negative impacts of marijuana on young people. He believes that focusing on preventing people under 21 from starting to use marijuana is the key next step. Califano suggests continuing to try to cut marijuana availability, but also treating youths arrested for marijuana possession, similar to what is done in drunk driving cases.

Califano is speaking about, not to, students of the same age as many of those you will be teaching. This assumed audience can be a good topic for discussion and may bother some students. Students may also have strong opinions one way or the other about marijuana use. The assumptions they come in with can be useful to add to the debate.

1. What positions, not necessarily stated by Califano, is he arguing against? What can you learn about the marijuana conversation from his article?
2. What does Califano argue should be done about marijuana regulation? What evidence does he use to back up these claims?
3. Who is Califano's target audience? How does his discussion of teenagers impact a teen audience possibly reading the article?
4. What are the main points of disagreement between Schlosser and Califano?

SCHLOSSER, "MAKE PEACE WITH POT"

Eric Schlosser argues that marijuana should be decriminalized in the United States. He points to examples in Canada where marijuana can be bought over-the-counter for medicinal purposes. Schlosser gives numerous statistics about the time, money, and other resources that go into regulating marijuana. He points out a focus on marijuana by the Bush administration, and says this focus is misplaced.

Schlosser does not argue that marijuana is completely safe, just that it causes fewer deaths than many other substances that receive vastly less money and attention. He suggests paying more attention to other nations that are reducing marijuana penalties. Schlosser suggests treating marijuana use like alcohol use—by rehabilitating rather than imprisoning.

Schlosser's article responds directly to issues in Califano's in some ways, but from a virtually opposite perspective. This provides a good opportunity to not only compare arguments but also to explore how greatly the assumptions one has coming into a debate shape the results of that debate.

1. What does Schlosser believe about marijuana use? What about marijuana regulation?
2. Why does Schlosser appeal to the examples of so many other nations? What are the main problems with marijuana regulation according to Schlosser?
3. Compare Schlosser and Califano's discussion of how to slow marijuana use, how to punish marijuana use, and the potential benefits of marijuana use.
4. Discuss Schlosser's use of statistics as a key form of evidence.
5. Compare the rhetorical strategies in Califano and Schlosser's articles. What sorts of arguments do they use to convince their audiences?
6. What are Schlosser's views of personal freedoms and the role of government regulation, based on this article?

ISSUE IN FOCUS: REGULATING TOBACCO

Discussions of tobacco regulation do not begin and end with age limits. There are also numerous regulations about advertising, such as no television ads and no ads that target children. Smoking is also prohibited in many indoor areas, including bars and restaurants in some cities. Even outdoor locations, such as bus stops in Portland, Oregon, have recently received new smoking limits.

The issue sometimes seems like smokers against non-smokers. Some want to be able to smoke, while others do not want to breathe in the secondhand smoke. Medical research about the dangers of secondhand smoke plays a key role in deciding where smoking is allowed. However, some of the debate is directly about when government regulation oversteps its bounds and enters into our private lives.

PHILLIP MORRIS, CAMEL LIGHTS AD AND AMERICAN LEGACY FOUNDA-
TION, ANTISMOKING AD

These advertisements show competing views of tobacco use that exist in society: smoking as an enjoyable companion to the leisure activity of cool people and smoking as a health risk that causes major, life-altering illnesses.

1. What are the arguments made in these advertisements? What evidence is used to support those arguments?
2. How do the visual elements of these two advertisements combine with the accompanying text to make arguments?
3. Why do people argue that Joe Camel was used to market cigarettes to minors? Can you find evidence to support this claim in the advertisement included here?

TRUDEAU, "THE SIN LOBBY GINS UP . . ."

This cartoon features one of Gary Trudeau's characteristic stylistic features in *Doonesbury*: the use of inanimate objects as stand-ins for people. In this case, a giant cigarette and joint represent industry lobbyists hobnobbing out on the town.

1. What argument is being made by this comic strip? What evidence supports that argument?
2. What is the "sin lobby"?
3. Compare the argument in this cartoon with those in Califano and Schlosser's essays. How are they different? The same? Which is the most compelling? Why?

BETTCHER AND SUBRAMANIAM, "THE NECESSITY OF GLOBAL TOBACCO REGULATIONS"

Bettcher and Subramaniam argue in this article that lax tobacco regulation in foreign countries allows tobacco companies to market and sell products containing dangerous levels of tar and nicotine. Because of this, they suggest that there should be international regulation of the tobacco industry.

1. What is the argument of this essay? What evidence is presented to support that argument?
2. Who is Bettcher and Subramaniam's audience? What effects might the authors' numerous citations have on the reader?
3. Bettcher and Subramaniam advocate for increased government control of tobacco, citing the health problems caused by tobacco products. Do you and your students find this evidence convincing? If not, what evidence would suggest the greater need for government control of tobacco?

WILLIAMS, "NAZI TACTICS"

In this article, Walter E. Williams claims that, prior to Hitler, Germany was largely a racially tolerant nation. What altered this situation was the successful deployment of Nazi propaganda which vilified the Jewish people. According to Williams, similar propaganda techniques are being used to vilify the tobacco industry and its primary product: cigarettes.

1. What is Williams's argument, and what evidence does he provide to support it?
2. Compare the view of government regulation in Williams' article to that of Bettcher and Subramaniam. Who is responsible for health and safety in their different arguments?
3. What is the effect of Williams references to the Nazis? How do these references fit (or fail to fit) with his audience's assumptions? What effect does it have on you as a reader?

GLADWELL, "DRUGSTORE ATHLETE" AND AMEND, "WHAT'S THIS?"

Malcolm Gladwell's "Drugstore Athlete" is an engaging consideration of both the ethics of using performance-enhancing drugs and the best means of addressing their increasingly prevalent use in competitive sports.

As Gladwell shows, the issue is highly complicated. Should sports officials attempt to prohibit the use of these drugs entirely, even though scientists' ability to test for them is limited at best? Or should officials seek to regulate the drugs' use in a way that protects athletes' safety and prevents the domination by those athletes who have access to the latest and most sophisticated pharmacology?

Gladwell's argument is largely evaluative. He shows that, despite what one may think, doping may not necessarily be all bad, and the current testing practices may be the best possible solution to the problem. Note Gladwell's concluding paragraphs, where he connects the use of performance-enhancing drugs to the use of plastic surgery, Prozac, and Ritalin. Gladwell suggests that athletes are no different from the rest of us. We all, in one way or another, seek to overcome physical limitations through pharmacology.

1. According to Gladwell, what are the problems with policies that prohibit entirely the use of performance-enhancing drugs?
2. Gladwell's style is so engaging that it's easy to overlook the bold claim he makes in his conclusion. Can we really compare an ADD sufferer's use of Ritalin with an athlete's use of steroids? Are these cases necessarily comparable?
3. How would you describe Gladwell's characteristic style and argumentative strategy?
4. What is the tone of the cartoon? How does it compare to the tone of Gladwell's essay? Do the two make similar arguments?

BÉRUBÉ, "CITIZENSHIP AND DISABILITY" AND BLITT, *NEW YORKER* COVER

In this article, Bérubé provides an update on the progress of his son, Jamie, who had been profiled in the author's book *Life as We Know It*. He then uses Jamie's example to launch into a discussion of the disabled and disability rights.

1. What is Bérubé's argument? What evidence does he supply to support that argument?
2. What is the overall impression of Jamie that you and your students get after reading Bérubé's description of him in paragraph 2? How does this impression challenge (or confirm) the way you typically think of "special" children?
3. What are the two conclusions that Bérubé arrives at in paragraph 11 after describing his experience watching Jamie grow up? Are these

conclusions arguments of some kind? If so, does the "evidence" of Jamie's life make them convincing?

4. What picture does Bérubé paint of the "politics" of disability? According to him, why are disability issues important to feminists and other progressives?

5. Examine Blitt's *New Yorker* cover. What meanings does it derive from its context, situated in the middle of Bérubé's article? What other meanings does it imply?

RAFFERTY, "KATE WINSLET, PLEASE SAVE US!"

Rafferty's essay is surprisingly challenging. Though he includes a number of witty observations and snarky asides, the heart of his argument—where he draws connections between stars, their bodies, and the eras in which they lived—is both compelling and ambitious.

You might use some clips from television and film while discussing this essay, if only to have specific examples available in class. As Rafferty suggests, you might compare Demi Moore and Madonna (at their most pumped-up) with Diana Rigg from "The Avengers." Have students read arguments regarding femininity, masculinity, strength, and sexuality in the voice of each actress (as well as their male counterparts). Alternatively, you might tell students that you plan to have a VCR or DVD player available in class on the day that you plan to discuss this essay. Invite students to bring their own tapes and disks in, so that they may present their own examples supporting or rebutting Rafferty's argument.

1. What is Rafferty's central claim here? Is this a casual argument, seeking a connection between stars' bodies and the time in which they live? Or is this ultimately a proposal argument, in which Rafferty calls for a change in Hollywood's conception of the ideal form?

2. As we note in the essay's head note, "Kate Winslet, Please Save Us!" first appeared in *GQ*. Are there places in this article where Rafferty seems to cater specifically to the needs, assumptions, and values of that magazine's readers? (You might bring a copy of the magazine to class so that students may examine its articles and advertising.) If this essay were transposed to a magazine for older readers, would Rafferty need to cut the second paragraph?

3. Are images of beauty tied, as Rafferty suggests, to larger issues in society and culture?

LEACH, "THOSE EXTRA POUNDS—ARE THEY GOVERNMENT'S BUSINESS?"

Susan Llewelyn Leach is concerned with the dissolving line between public and private. Specifically, she does not want anti-obesity campaigns to make what people eat a public issue. She cites multiple researchers to show that when "social disapproval" becomes strong, that issue tends to become public. Also, the projected economic costs related to obesity have made the federal government quite interested. However, obesity is not always a food problem, the reasons for obesity are many, and often are not under an individual's direct control.

According to Leach, societal pressure and economic issues are the two main factors leading to new or additional government regulation. She argues that in the case of obesity, neither of these are very sound reasons. Economic figures are hard to determine, and obesity gets blamed for many more medical issues than it is responsible for, according to Sandle Sabo-Russo. Leach quotes those who are worried that legislation will go too far on obesity issues.

1. What is Leach's view of obesity regulation? How can you tell her view from that of the people she quotes? What various opinions that disagree with Leach are in her article?
2. Examine the use of quotes in this essay. How do these quotes help make logos, pathos, or ethos arguments?
3. According to Leach, what are the main causes of further government regulation for a substance or issue? What evidence is given for this? What counterarguments can you think of?
4. What does Leach mean by "demonized" in this article? What is "demonized" and what results come of that?
5. In what ways is obesity an economic issue?

UDOVITCH, "A SECRET SOCIETY OF THE STARVING"

This article profiles the "pro-ana" movement which champions eating disorders like anorexia and bulimia as legitimate "lifestyle choices." Udovitch interviews several women who are prominent participants on pro-ana Web sites, noting the ways that these women operate in society and use the Internet to fuel and publicize their behavior.

1. What is Udovitch's argument? What evidence is there to support that argument?
2. Is Udovitch's introduction to "Claire" effective in making her argument? Why does the author present her subject, and the town she lives in, in this particular way?
3. According to Udovitch, pro-ana individuals argue that anorexia is a "lifestyle choice," not a disease. What is at stake in re-naming the behaviors that make up anorexia in this way? In changing its status from a disease to an acceptable way of life?
4. In paragraph 28, Udovitch writes that the Internet is a place where a girl who "hates herself . . . can make her internal state external." What does this mean? How does this description of the Internet relate to your own experience?

CONSUMER FREEDOM, OBESITY AD

The two ads from Consumer Freedom argue that the standards for measuring obesity are flawed. Furthermore, they argue that obesity is a matter of personal choices and responsibility, not something for the government to be focusing on. In the upper left ad, they use visual and written counterexamples, naming people who seem to be obviously fit and healthy, but who are considered obese by federal standards. In the lower right ad, they again use a seemingly ridiculous case of blaming others, and phrase it as a joke, to argue for personal responsibility.

1. How would you describe the role of the pictures compared to the text in each ad? Are the pictures used differently in these two ads?
2. What is Consumer Freedom arguing for? How do the arguments differ slightly in these two ads?

3. Who does it seem like these ads are representing? Who probably supports Consumer Freedom?
4. What are these ads arguing against? Where can you think of that they would be likely to appear?

WYSONG, "MODIFIED" AND LEWIS, "THE SUBTEXT OF ALL TATTOOS"

In this article aimed at pre-teen and teenaged readers, Wysong outlines the medical and other complications that can come with tattoos and body piercing.

1. What is Wysong's argument, and what evidence does she provide to support that argument?
2. How would you characterize the tone of Wysong's essay? Is it effective for her intended audience?
3. Is Wysong for or against tattoos and piercings?
4. How are the two arguments—in Wysong and the comic—different? How are they the same?

MOTHERS AGAINST DRUNK DRIVING, ANTI-DRINKING AND DRIVING AD, "LIKE FATHER, LIKE SON"

This advertisement from Mothers against Drunk Driving shows a father and son in the same position, drinking a beer behind the wheel of a car. The ad targets parents whom MADD believes should think about the messages they give to their children about drinking. There is a fair amount of text under the picture, directed toward fathers in particular, reminding them that "kids imitate their parents."

1. What specific visual details stand out most to you? What impression do you get just from the pictures?
2. How do the text and the images relate to each other? How do the three different sections of text connect to each other?
3. Identify any pathos, logos, and ethos arguments you find in this ad.
4. Whom do you think the main target audience for this ad is?

KINZIE, "A RARE KIND OF RUSH: A SORORITY BASED ON IS-LAMIC PRINCIPLES"

Susan Kinzie describes the women of Gamma Gamma Chi, a national sorority for Islamic women. The goal of the group is to challenge stereotypes about Muslims by utilizing sororities' traditional emphasis on community outreach to bring Islamic women into greater contact with other groups on and around college campuses.

1. What is Kinzie's argument? What evidence does she supply to support that argument?
2. Why does the idea of a Muslim sorority seem odd? What is it about sororities that seems so different from Muslim life? Why does this not seem to be the case with other identity-based sororities? How are the two cultures likely to affect each other?
3. What positive influences might Muslim culture have on Greek-life culture? Is it likely that a Muslim sorority will lead to the wider understanding of Muslims and elimination of prejudices that some of the sorority members believe?

IN-CLASS ACTIVITIES

• Discuss the character of Joe Camel with your students. What do they know about that character? As a group, perform a visual analysis of the ad. What argument is his ad making? How does the Surgeon General's warning impact the ad?

• Describe the relationships between the images and text in the Legacy ad and the Doonesbury cartoon. What arguments are these items making? What role does pathos play in these two visuals? Once you and your students have identified the arguments in the two visuals, work as a group on outlining a short written version of one of the arguments. When you are finished, compare your written version with the original image. What benefits are there to the visual version? The textual one? Which seems more persuasive? Why?

• As a class, examine an issue of the *New Yorker*. You may be able to check out several copies of the publication from your library; alternatively, if you meet in a computer-enabled classroom, you could examine newyorker.com. After completing this examination with your students, try to explain the audience for the magazine, then connect that explanation to Gladwell's arguments. How does he try to appeal to that audience? Challenge it?

• Have your students watch the video "Women in Film" (available on YouTube or here: http://viz.cwrl.utexas.edu/node/178) as a companion to Rafferty's article. Have them perform a short visual analysis of the video. What arguments does it make? How does it make those arguments? Do they confirm or contradict Rafferty's argument?

• Divide your students into small groups, and have the groups find several measures or definitions of obesity, and then write a review of how obesity is being defined. Consider putting a variety of definitions into two or three general categories. Then have them draft a short argument for their own definition of obesity and present it to the class.

• As a group, analyze Consumer Freedom and what they stand for based on the ads in this chapter (or you could visit their Web site for more information about the group).

SHORT ASSIGNMENTS

• Take the information from Califano's essay and write a version of it for a different audience (perhaps for parents of grade-schoolers or for 15 year olds).

• Write a proposal for what should be done about marijuana regulation that considers both Schlosser and Califano as part of the audience.

• Create an ad promoting some form of tobacco regulation. Create a countering ad that promotes freedom for smokers.

• In a short paper, have your students choose three major pathos arguments from the "Issue in Focus" section, describe each, show the context for each, and discuss their roles in the overall arguments being made.

• Have your students write a short rebuttal to either Bettcher and Subramaniam or Williams and then propose an alternate solution to the problem introduced by that article.

• Have your students find an essay that they've already written and submitted, either from this class or some other, then revise that essay so that it's written in Gladwell's characteristic style.

• Choose an issue from this chapter, and write a testimony to give before a congressional committee on that issue. Be sure to consider how to phrase your texts for a spoken context and to consider the congressional audience. In preparation for this assignment, you might find the text of a recent congressional testimony (perhaps on steroids in baseball) and share it with your students.

• In a short essay, have your students rebut one or several of Rafferty's claims. Perhaps you think that Demi Moore's portrayal of a Navy SEAL was empowering for women. Or perhaps you feel that Diana Rigg's Emma Peel ultimately promoted an unhealthy model of femininity. Don't try to address every one of Rafferty's arguments. Focus on one and then provide evidence supporting your counterclaim.

• How might one of the other writers whose work is included in this section respond to Rafferty's argument? Write a letter to Rafferty in the voice of Malcolm Gladwell, Mim Udovitch, or Susan Kinzie. Respond to any aspect of Rafferty's essay—its central claims, its rhetorical purpose, its style, its place of publication (and how its publication may have compromised the effectiveness of his argument).

• Overall, Leach's article provides warnings against too much regulation of food and obesity. Only using quotes from her article, write your own that is more in favor of regulation (or even more strongly against it).

• Alone or in small groups, have your students create an ad with the same style used by the two Consumer Freedom ads.

Chapter 28: New Media

The popularity of self publishing on the Internet has made it possible to mass-distribute information in ways that circumvent the influence of the mass media. The use of multimedia communication on the Internet has been referred to as "new media," a term that is suggestive not only of the new forms of media available to both users and consumers, but also of the challenge that this new media represents to old media; that is, to the old, hierarchical model of media distribution.

According to Lev Manovich in *The New Media Reader* (MIT Press, 2003), "new media are the cultural objects which use digital computer technology for distribution and exhibition." While your students may not be familiar with the term "new media," it is likely that they are familiar with new media itself, in the form of Web publishing, online video, social networking, and video games. The essays included in this chapter discuss the role of these new media in society, both positively and negatively. By drawing on your students' experiences with digital publishing, and by providing them with new experiences using the sample activities and assignments at the end of the chapter, you will have a greater chance of engaging your students with the politics and ideas that inform the new media landscape.

KEEN, "IS GOOGLE'S DATA GRINDER DANGEROUS?"

In this short article, Keen outlines Google's plans for iGoogle, a personal Internet service. As the world's leading Internet search engine, Google already controls much of the traffic on the Internet, and Keen suggests that this bid for more "eyeballs" is not an altruistic one, despite the company's desire to suggest otherwise.

1. What is Keen's argument? What evidence is used to support it?
2. What sort of appeal—ethos, pathos, logos—does Keen primarily rely on in this essay? How does the answer to this question affect your reading of the essay?

3. What kind of "danger" does Google represent to society? How is this danger different from other problems society must confront?
4. If your students aren't aware of the details of *1984*, give them a quick summary of the book, particularly the significance of Room 101. Is Keen's comparison between information services like iGoogle and Room 101 a good one? How does Room 101 relate to Keen's suggestion in paragraph 5 that iGoogle and similar services will lead to the denial of individual responsibility?

BARLOW, "A DECLARATION OF THE INDEPENDENCE OF CYBERSPACE"

John Perry Barlow's mystical "Declaration" includes many of the arguments about cyberspace that "netizens" have been making for years. Like many of these long-term cyberspace dwellers, Barlow refuses to accept outside regulation. In his "Declaration," he links himself with the early American patriots in an attempt to construct a new society, what he calls a "Civilization of the Mind in Cyberspace."

Barlow's argument proceeds from a definitional claim—that cyberspace is a kind of virtual country, the "new home of Mind." It "consists of transactions, relationships, and thought itself . . . . Ours is a world that is both everywhere and nowhere, but it is not where bodies live."

1. List the comparisons that Barlow's essay implies between cyberspace and the physical world. What characterizes this world of "flesh and steel"? How is cyberspace different?
2. Does the Internet really exist in a realm beyond the material world? To what extent may it be characterized as another "country"? Is there a point where that comparison breaks down?
3. To what extent does Barlow's argument rely on emotional appeals? Which of his readers' assumptions and values does he hope to tap in to?
4. Do you agree with Barlow's sense that cyberspace may become "more humane and fair" than the material world?
5. How does Barlow associate himself with the figures of American history? What purpose does this association serve? What is the effect of this association?

6. What might this "Civilization of the Mind in Cyberspace" look like? Is it in the process of being created? How has the Internet altered the products of human creativity?

SEIGENTHALER, "A FALSE WIKIPEDIA 'BIOGRAPHY' "

In this "highly personal story," Seigenthaler recounts his experience being defamed in the Internet encyclopedia, Wikipedia. Seigenthaler recounts his discovery of the defaming remarks—which suggested he was a suspect in the assassinations of President John F. Kennedy and his brother Robert Kennedy—and his subsequent, frustrating efforts to find and hold responsible the person (or persons) who wrote these remarks.

1. What is Seigenthaler's argument? What evidence does he use to support it?
2. What qualities of narrative argument does Seigenthaler's essay showcase? How would the effect of this essay change if it were a proposal or causation argument?
3. Is Seigenthaler's story one that is applicable to a wider audience? Does it suggest a proposal for change in the freedom of individuals to post and consume new media?
4. What does this essay imply about Wikipedia's value as a source of information? How does this implication jibe with you or your students' own experiences with the encyclopedia?

HANDELSMAN, "INFORMATION SUPERHIGHWAY"

Walt Handelsman's editorial cartoon responds to the overblown, utopian rhetoric of many concerning the Internet. The Web provides increasingly easy access to all sorts of information, including pornography. And as Handelsman suggests, porn remains some of the Web's most popular content.

1. What is Handelsman's central claim? Does he have several central claims?
2. Why is "sex" portrayed as an offramp?
3. What other visual features of the comic stand out? Why are they important?

GERSON, "WHERE THE AVATARS ROAM"

This essay by political writer Michael Gerson suggests that the behavior of users in online, virtual communities are governed by political forces, just as they are in the real world. According to him, primary political philosophy of the Second Life virtual environment is libertarianism, a philosophy which he believes lessens users' sense of personal and social responsibility and leads to disorder.

1. What is Gerson's central claim? What evidence does he supply to support it?
2. If your students aren't familiar with libertarianism, provide them with a short description of this political theory. Then, discuss with them Gerson's description of Second Life as a "large-scale experiment in libertarianism."
3. Discuss with your students Gerson's claim that the unrestrained freedom of Second Life is like a "seedy, derelict carnival." Are there any positive uses of the service that you can think of? How might those positive uses challenge Gerson's negative portrayal of the service?
4. Gerson suggests that society flounders without a moral code. If such a code were to be applied to cyberspace, which crosses many cultural and national boundaries, whose code would it be? Who would get to decide which code applies?

BENNETT AND BEITH, "ALTERNATE UNIVERSE"

In this essay, Bennett and Beith respond more positively to Second Life than Gerson does. They describe the origins of the site, outlining its economic impact, as well as the way it accommodates "the gamut of human activities." They find Second Life to be a mostly positive cultural influence, one which allows for interactions between users spread across the globe, new marketing and economic opportunities for businesses, and the overall empowerment of users.

1. What is the argument of this essay? What evidence does it contain?
2. How do Bennett and Beith depict the avatar-driven world of Second Life differently from Gerson? Does the word 'avatar' have different connotations in the two essays?

147

3. Who do you think is the audience for this essay? For Gerson's essay

4. This essay depicts both the positive and negative aspects of life in Second Life. What is the effect of this presentation, compared to Gerson's essay?

5. What is Bennett and Beith's reaction to the politics inherent in Second Life?

FISCHLER, "PUTTING ON LIP GLOSS, AND A SHOW, FOR YOU-TUBE VIEWERS"

In this article, Fischler describes the YouTube phenomenon of home-made "how-to" videos. She interviews users who create short programs discussing everything from the basics of putting on makeup to arranging flowers.

1. What is Fischler's central claim? What evidence does he supply to support it?

2. There are several places in this article where YouTube users explain why they use the site and what the exposure it brings them means to them personally. Identify a few of these comments with your students and use them as a basis of discussing the impact of online video, not just for making money, but for personal expression.

3. In paragraph 7, a sociology professor remarks that "YouTube is an obvious place for formerly private acts to be made public." Why is this "obvious"? What are some possible long-term effects of private acts being made public?

4. If it is possible, show your class 1–2 of the videos mentioned in this article. How does Fischler's descriptions of those videos match your or your students' experience in viewing them? Does viewing these videos in conjunction with reading the essay strengthen Fischler's argument? Weaken it? Why?

DUFFY AND KEEN, "CAN ANYONE BE A DESIGNER?"

Against the background of the current trend of democratizing content creation that exists on the Internet and elsewhere, Duffy and Keen debate the question of whether anyone should be able to call him- or herself a designer. Duffy advocates for broadening this term to include everyone, while Keen argues that it should be reserved for design professionals.

1. What are Duffy and Keen's arguments in this conversation? What evidence is given to support those arguments?
2. Who is more persuasive in this dialogue, Duffy or Keen (or is it a draw)? Have your students explain their answers in reference to rhetorical features like ethos, pathos, logos, style, and tone.
3. In paragraph 5, Keen refers to Duffy's statement "Make design part of everyday life" as being "Utopian" and "Ministry of Truth-ish." Look up the definitions of these terms (the first was coined by Thomas More for his eponymous book and the second by George Orwell in *1984*) with your students. Are they apt? What is Keen saying about Duffy's vision of design by using these terms? Compare these references to Keen's allusions to *1984* in his essay.

BOYD, "FACEBOOK'S PRIVACY TRAINWRECK: EXPOSURE, IN-VASION, AND SOCIAL CONVERGENCE"

In this journal article, boyd describes the fallout related to the introduction of "News Feeds" on the social networking site Facebook. She then uses this example to prompt a discussion of what counts as privacy online and to compare and contrast the social relationships that exist on- and offline

1. What is boyd's argument, and what evidence does she provide to support it?
2. Have your students perform a visual analysis of the two images of the founders of MySpace and Facebook. What is different about the images? Their settings, backgrounds, composition, "models"?
3. Williams claims in paragraph 4 of her essay that "The tech world" sees privacy as a binary—either something is private, or it is public. What different view of privacy does she argue for? Do you or your students agree with this view?
4. How does the use of the term "friend" on social networking sites like MySpace and Facebook differ from our use of the word in other social contexts? How does this difference cause problems for some users?

5. At the beginning of her article, boyd connects the introduction of search to Usenet with the introduction of News Feeds to Facebook. Many theorists speculate that the future of Internet search lies in mining the social information connecting users on sites like Facebook. Do the issues that boyd raises in this article make this impending "social search" seem troubling? Exciting? Some combination of the two?

WILLIAMS, "GETTING OFF THE COUCH"

Stephen Williams documents the phenomenal success of Nintendo's Wii game platform, which has become a hit with individuals who would not normally consider themselves video-game players. One reason for this success is that the Wii's primary interface is a motion-sensing controller that requires the full-bodied participation of players, challenging the typical image of video gaming as a sedentary activity.

1. What is Williams's argument, and what evidence does he provide to support it?
2. How does characterizing a video game system as being "exercise" change the way video games are typically viewed? What is at stake in combining these typically antithetical activities? Is there a "rhetoric of video gaming" which is challenged by this definition?
3. Is the Wii really a video game system in the sense that the Playstation 3 is a video game system? (Each offer very different games and different technical capabilities.) What would be the effect of Nintendo re-branding the Wii as an "interactive exercise video"? Again, how does the Wii challenge traditional definitions of video gaming?

IN-CLASS ACTIVITIES

• Have your students write brief reviews of Handelsman's cartoon as if they were members of the ACLU and share them with the rest of the class.

• Have your students bring in examples of editorial cartoons (examples can be found in a local newspaper or at http://cartoonbox.slate.com). As a class, survey everyone's selected cartoons, paying close attention to the individual strengths and weaknesses of each. Finally, either on the board or in some other forum accessible to the class, outline the features of effective editorial cartoons. For example, try to pinpoint what makes them funny or not, or what techniques are effective or not.

• Find an editorial cartoon and assess its effectiveness as an argument. What is its central claim? How does it make its case? Who is its intended audience? Does it convince its audience of its argument?

• If you have access to computers in your classroom, visit the Wikipedia page for a person or topic that would be familiar to the class (an author or work studied in class, for example). See if there are any errors or omissions that the group can identify. If so, correct them as a class. Later visit the page and see if the corrections have been altered by other users.

• Have your students break up into small groups of 1–2 and have them choose an article in an encyclopedia. (If you have access to computers in your class, you can probably access an encyclopedia from your library's online databases; otherwise, you might choose and print out some of those database articles or photocopy articles from a print encyclopedia for this exercise.) Have the students compare that article with the Wikipedia article on the same topic, focusing on each article's tone, and the selection of information they contain. Which is more encyclopedic? Which has a better ethos? At the end of the exercise, have your students briefly share their results with the rest of the class.

If you have the time, prepare a list of topics yourself, and find the corresponding Wikipedia and print encyclopedia articles online. Then, run the text of each article through a word processor (cut and paste the online text, removing any distinctive formatting and attributions) so that students can't identify its origin as coming from Wikipedia or from a print source. Then ask them to identify which article in a pair is the most "encyclopedic," and have them justify their answers with specific examples from the texts.

• While your class is reading Keen's dialogue with Duffy, browse through a week or so of posts on the MAKE blog (blog.makezine.com) with your students. (*MAKE* is a magazine published for the do-it-yourself crowd, people who like to design and build their own mechanical and technological objects. The blog is devoted to the same topic and highlights the projects of "makers" who read and contribute to the magazine.) Have your students choose 1–2 posts on the blog and analyze them in light of this dialogue. Have them briefly discuss the projects they have chosen with the rest of the class, focusing on how those projects affect their reaction to Keen and Duffy's arguments.

SHORT ASSIGNMENTS

• Barlow describes cyberspace as a "contagion." How is it a "contagion?" What is the nature of the contagion? Why use a negative word for something that Barlow obviously supports? Write a definitional essay affirming or contradicting Barlow's argument that cyberspace is a contagion.

• Revise Barlow's argument so that it makes its central definitional claim more explicitly. Emphasize logical appeals rather than emotional ones.

• If your students have access to the required technology, assign them to sign up for free Second Life accounts and to then explore the service for a week. Then, have them write a short essay where they either engage Gerson's negative portrayal of the service or Bennett and Beith's more positive one. Does their experience suggest that the chosen portrayal is a correct one? Why or why not?

• Have your students choose a public profile from MySpace and write a short analysis of that profile, taking into account the visual, auditory, and textual elements that exist on the page. Have them take a special look at the empowering aspects of that person's presentation of him or herself (à la Fischler) as well as the privacy issues related to that presentation (à la Boyd).

• Have your students find a YouTube user who regularly posts videos of him or herself to the site and then view 3–5 of that user's videos. Instruct them to write a 1–2 page analysis of those videos based on the goals of the users described in Fischler's article.

• At the end of 2007, Facebook introduced "Beacon," an ad-delivery system that showed users' purchases from external Web sites in their News Feeds. The user reaction was similar to the introduction of News Feeds; users hated Beacon. Have your students read the company's reaction to

152

this backlash on the Facebook blog (http://blog.facebook.com/blog.php?post=7584397130) and then write a 1–2 page rhetorical analysis of this response.

• If you are reading fictional texts in your class, assign your students a character from that text and have them create a MySpace page for that character. Instruct them to choose the layout, design, and other elements of the page based on how their assigned character might be expected to design their profile. Have your students share their character profiles with each other in class. If you would like to extend the assignment, have students impersonate the characters and interact with each other through the social networking site. At the end of the assignment, have them talk about the choices they have made for their characters and how those choices are based on the actions of the character in the original text.

• Have your students search for "Wii users" or "Wii user" on Google image search (images.google.com). Then, have them select 1–2 of the most interesting images they find and write a short visual analysis of each one. Finally, have students present their images and analysis to the rest of the class, either in person or in an online forum accessible to other class members.

Building Your Course

This section of the manual includes sample handouts you can consult when creating your own assignments and syllabi. As always, we hope that you find these examples helpful, either as models for your own materials, or as tools that you use when creating or revising other kinds of handouts and assignments.

One distinctive feature of these assignments is that they are designed to evaluate the different stages of the writing process, and, in doing so, encourage your students to think about and engage with this process. This design allows you to intervene at crucial points in the writing process, offering advice, encouragement, and when necessary, correction. It is equally important that this design requires students to think of their writing assignments as extended projects in which they propose, compose, and revise their arguments. At every opportunity, remind your students that this understanding of writing and making arguments is one that they should apply to other writing tasks, whether in their other courses, the workplace, or their lives as citizens in a participatory democracy.

How does this pedagogical strategy affect your work as an instructor? It means that you will likely require students to complete and submit topic proposals for their major assignments and require multiple submissions of those assignments. It means that you will read a lot of your students' work, and that as a reader you will play a number of different roles, such as audience member, coach, or devil's advocate. Finally, it means that your students will need clear instructions—probably written instructions—to guide them as they move through the different stages of their assignments.

TOPIC PROPOSALS

What is a topic proposal? Put simply, it is a tentative sketch of the student's plan for his or her essay—what it's about, who it's for, why it's important, what its purposes are, and how the student plans to accomplish those purposes. We ask our students to complete topic proposals for each of the major essays they write.

Some instructors ask their students to write their proposals in paragraph form. Other instructors create topic proposal worksheets that require students to answer pointed questions about their project, such as: Who is your audience? What do you hope to convince them of? Why should your argument be important to them? What problems do you expect to encounter when writing the essay? Both of these formats can be successful. Whatever you do, impress upon your students the importance of these proposals. And make sure that your students understand that the topic proposal only *begins* the process of making an argument. It is likely that, in the course of writing their draft, their audience or purpose will change entirely. But they should never lose sight of the proposal's core concerns: thesis, audience, exigence, purpose, and argumentative strategy.

Offer guidance when responding to proposals. Also, don't be afraid to make a student rewrite a topic proposal, or to count hastily completed proposals as incomplete. In such cases, explain to students that they aren't yet prepared to begin a draft. Also, don't be afraid to warn students away from a topic, or to steer them toward a related but more manageable one. Don't allow them to go ahead with a draft that's sure to cause them more trouble than they can handle in the time allotted for the assignment.

INITIAL SUBMISSIONS

You and your students should be in agreement about what makes the initial submission of a paper "complete." Before students submit their papers for the first time, you should discuss with them what their goals are for these submissions. While you are free to design your assignments as you see fit, generally, we expect initial submissions to make a claim supported by good reasons and evidence. We expect a student to have thought carefully about the topic and goals of the paper and to have drafted the submission accordingly. Finally, we expect a first submission to be typed and double-spaced, with ample margins in which you and their peers can write comments.

We generally provide extensive comments on all submissions before the final one. Students need detailed feedback at this stage in their writing process in order to give them direction in completing later revisions. In our responses, we use several voices: we speak as teachers, focusing on the concepts covered in class. We speak as coaches, supporting students in their efforts to master certain concepts, skills, or practices. Finally, we speak as readers, responding as best we can as members of the target audience. It's up to you to balance these roles effectively.

One final word of advice: talk openly with your students about your responses to their work. Explain to them what your goals are in responding to each of their assignments. When reading a topic proposal, do you read for the same things that you would while reading a final submission? On what level do you expect to engage them in their initial submissions? Also, make sure students understand how to *use* your comments. For instance, should they address only those parts of the essay that you've commented on, or are they expected to make holistic revisions?

FINAL SUBMISSIONS

As with initial submissions, make sure your students know what the requirements of a final submission are and the criteria that you will use in assessing them. (See the model assignment sheets for examples.)

When responding to final submissions, we generally don't make extensive comments. We have before us not only the initial and final submissions (and any submissions in between) but also the self-assessment, the peer review, and the revision record. Therefore, the comments we make are general ones, addressing the quality and strategy of a student's argument, his or her work on the essay, and his or her own sense of its success. Whenever possible, we try to make connections to the next essay assignment, or at the end of the term, to the student's development as a writer over the past several months.

Students know that a final submission is final: this is the essay that gets the grade. Even so, encourage your students to think beyond their final submissions, and to see their writing as something that evolves long after they complete their assignments.

Rhetorical Analysis

The rhetorical analysis is an especially effective first essay. The assignment requires students to assess a persuasive text's effectiveness as a piece of rhetoric. You may ask them to choose to write either a *textual* rhetorical analysis or a *contextual* rhetorical analysis, or a combination of the two. In the first instance, they will be identifying and commenting on how well the text uses pathetic, ethical, and logical appeals to convince a particular audience of its argument. You may also ask them to comment on the arrangement and style of the given piece. In the second instance, they will be evaluating the strength of the text according to the circumstances surrounding its publication (including its material appearance or where or how the argument appears), and the larger political or historical or social conversations in which it participates.

You can conduct this assignment in a number of ways. If you have your students find their own texts to analyze—as our assignment sheet does—make sure that the students select something *current*. You might even stipulate that the text be no more than three weeks old. As an alternative, you might provide students with 2–3 texts from which they may choose. That way, the students can discuss each text in class (and you will have the benefit of not having to read all of their source texts). And because they will have read each of these texts, their peer review sessions might be more lively and substantive.

By customizing your assignment, you also discourage plagiarism. Assignments that ask students to choose their own articles and then write on them are fairly common and can be bought on the many Web sites now devoted to selling student papers. If you tailor this assignment to your course's specific topic and goals, those students who might be inclined to buy or borrow their papers will have an especially hard time finding something that will work. You may also talk with your campus librarians about the resources they have compiled to assist you in combating plagiarism.

Model Assignment Sheet: Rhetorical Analysis

Choose a recently published newspaper editorial or column and assess whether it persuades its audience of its central claim and reasons. Your essay should identify at the outset the audience at which the piece is aimed, its argumentative purpose, and its central argument. Once you have identified these concerns, evaluate the rhetorical effectiveness of the given text according to either a *textual* rhetorical analysis *or* a *contextual* rhetorical analysis:

1. *Textual* rhetorical analysis: examine i) the writer's use of the three rhetorical appeals (ethos, pathos, and logos); ii) the arrangement and style of the given piece.
2. *Contextual* rhetorical analysis: examine i) the effectiveness of argument according to how it appears or is "packaged" (the form or type of publication in which it appears); ii) the author of the given text, and other writings he or she has produced, and how this information plays a role in your evaluation of the text; iii) 1–2 larger political or social conversations that the text seems to be participating in or contributing to, and if the text makes a significant contribution to those conversations.

The paper should be three to five pages long, typed, double-spaced, and carefully proofread.

GRADING CRITERIA

I will evaluate your essay according to these criteria:

- Clear identification of your chosen text's argument, argumentative purpose, and rhetorical context
- Demonstrated understanding of the basics of arguments, as they are presented in Part 1 of *Good Reasons with Contemporary Arguments*

- Effective essay structure
- Clear and precise sentence-level rhetoric (grammar and style)

TIPS AND REMINDERS

In this essay, you will take a stand on whether or not the editorial you've chosen persuades its audience of its central argument. This essay, then, is *not* primarily about the issue or subject discussed in the editorial. It is instead about the rhetorical strategy the writer employs.

Remember that any successful argument makes a central claim and then supports that claim with good reasons. Use the "Steps to Writing a Rhetorical Analysis" in Chapter 5 to develop your argument.

Be sure to back up your comments with specific details from the text. In other words, support what you're saying with summaries, paraphrases, and quotes from the text. Use the information presented in Chapter 19 of *Good Reasons with Contemporary Arguments* as a guide in using sources effectively.

TOPIC PROPOSAL

Your topic proposal should describe the text you choose to write about. You should mention where and when the piece was published, summarize its central argument, and identify its intended audience. The proposal should also state your central claim regarding the success of the editorial's argument and your reasons supporting this claim. Your topic proposal should be one paragraph long and carefully proofread.

Definition Argument

At the end of term, students often tell us that the definition argument was the most difficult assignment of the course. They report that they had trouble finding a good topic, establishing convincing criteria, and explaining the significance of their issue and claim to their audience. Many say that they did not really "get" the definitional argument until later in the course, after they had completed several other assignments.

These difficulties may have as much to do with the way we order our assignments as with the nature of definition arguments. Generally, we find that students struggle most with the second essay of the term, whatever it involves. Why? At that point, students have just received their first graded essays and are trying to incorporate a number of new terms, concepts, and approaches into their work. Still, definition arguments *are* hard to conceive and write. Therefore, it is especially important to keep an eye on your students as they develop their definition arguments. Pay special attention to their topic proposals, because the way in which they word their claims is especially important. (Students can often unknowingly change definitional claims into evaluative claims.) You may have to meet with students early in the composition process to help them get their essays off the ground. Ask each student: Is this an arguable claim? Who is the audience, and why is this definitional issue of concern to them? How do you plan to develop and support your criteria? How will you strengthen your own ethos? Once students begin drafting, watch for potential problems and try to catch them before they veer off course.

Consider teaching definition arguments along with the chapters in *Good Reasons with Contemporary Arguments* dealing with effective research and documentation. In a definition argument, you argue for your criteria as well as your central claim, and often you require sources in doing both. This may well be the essay in which students rely most heavily on secondary sources from the library. (Note: in our model assignment sheet, we require that students use at least three sources.)

Model Assignment Sheet: Definition Argument

Write a definitional argument in order to take a stand on a controversial issue. Your definitional claim may use the following formula:

> **X** is (or is not) a **Y** because it has (or does not have) features **A, B, C**. . .

Examples:

- Nutrition bars are (or are not) a form of candy bar, because. . .

- Keeping animals in zoos is (or is not) a form of cruelty to animals, because. . .

- Cheerleading is (or is not) a sport, because. . .

You should choose a particular audience and develop your argument for its members. Ask yourself, to whom does this definitional issue—and your argument—matter? Craft your essay so that its pathetic, ethical, and logical appeals are appropriate to these readers.

You must use three or more secondary sources in your essay. Make sure that these sources are chosen and employed with your audience in mind.

Your essay should be three to five pages long, typed, double-spaced, and carefully proofread. You should format your essay according to MLA (or APA) guidelines and include a Works Cited page.

GRADING CRITERIA

I will evaluate your essay according to these criteria:

- Development of an arguable definitional claim

- Demonstrated understanding of definition arguments as they are presented in Chapter 8 of *Good Reasons*

- Thorough consideration of your audience and effective employment of strategies designed to persuade them

- Effective essay structure
- Effective use, citation, and documentation of source material
- Clear and precise sentence-level rhetoric (grammar and style)
- Adherence to MLA (or APA) formatting guidelines, as presented in *Good Reasons with Contemporary Arguments*, Chapters 20–21

TIPS AND REMINDERS

Review "Steps to a Definition Argument" in Chapter 8 of *Good Reasons with Contemporary Arguments*.

Make sure that your claim is arguable. Can your X term be easily included in the category represented by your Y term? Is your Y term an arguable case?

At some point in your essay, you will need to explain to your readers why you think it is important to define the term you have chosen. What are the implications of your claim? Make certain to make clear why your readers should care about the topic and give them enough information to understand your position.

Use sources that your audience will consider reliable. Source material should contribute something to your paper that you cannot: specific facts, clarification or emphasis of a point, a voice with authority in a specific area, or illustration of the controversy or complexity of your issue.

TOPIC PROPOSAL

For your topic proposal, answer each of these questions as completely as possible.

- What is your definitional claim?
- Who is your audience? Why should your claim matter to them? How will this audience's needs and assumptions shape your argumentative strategy?
- What criteria will you use to define your Y term?

- With what authority will you establish these criteria?

- What problems or challenges do you foresee in writing this essay?

Evaluation Argument

After completing their definitional arguments, students find evaluation arguments a welcome relief. In this assignment, their goal is not to find the criteria defining a certain class or category, but instead to determine what makes something better or worse than other members of its class. This is no easy task. Still, to use a common example, it is easier perhaps to explain what makes a poem good than it is to determine what makes something a poem.

We generally assign an evaluation argument in the unit in which we also cover the basics of visual rhetoric. Hence, the assignment that follows requires students to write a review of a Web site. Students must make an evaluation argument that draws on the material presented in *Good Reasons,* Chapter 6. Alternatively, you might have your students write a movie or book review, or an assessment of a work of art or architecture on campus. Perhaps they can develop a Web site rather than an essay as their final draft. In any case, we have found that this unit is especially amenable to discussions of visual rhetoric. Consider what will work best with your own students and campus resources.

The section titled "Steps to Evaluation Argument" in Chapter 10 of *Good Reasons* offers other assignments that you might consider. Some of these assignments, unlike the assignment offered here, require students to engage more with their local surroundings. Requiring students to assess the effectiveness of their particular academic program, to review a local Mexican restaurant, or to evaluate a certain school policy gets them more involved in their campus community. We recommend these assignments, too. They may not encourage discussion of visual rhetoric, but they certainly offer you the opportunity to make connections between what they're learning in your class and what they're doing in their lives outside the classroom.

Model Assignment Sheet: Evaluation Argument

Write a review of a Web site in the form of an evaluation argument. Your essay may use this formula:

> **X** is a good (bad, the best, the worst, etc.) **Y** if measured by certain criteria **A, B, C**. . .

Examples:

- Moveon.org has an outstanding campaign Web site because. . .

- *Salon* is the best general-interest online magazine because. . .

Your evaluation should take into account the material dealing with effective visual design and effective Web design presented in Chapter 6 of *Good Reasons with Contemporary Arguments*.

Your paper should be three to five pages long, typed, double-spaced, and carefully proofread. You should use MLA (or APA) guidelines for formatting and include a Works Cited page.

GRADING CRITERIA

I will evaluate your essay according to these criteria:

- Development of an evaluative claim

- Demonstrated understanding of evaluation arguments, as explained in *Good Reasons*, Chapter 10

- Demonstrated understanding of effective visual design, as explained in *Good Reasons*, Chapter 6

- Thorough consideration of your audience and effective employment of strategies designed to persuade them

- Effective essay structure

- Effective use, citation, and documentation of source material

- Clear and precise sentence-level rhetoric (grammar and style)
- Adherence to MLA (or APA) formatting guidelines, as presented in *Good Reasons*, Chapters 20–21

TIPS AND REMINDERS

Review "Steps to an Evaluation Argument" in *Good Reasons with Contemporary Arguments*, Chapter 10. Make sure your claim is arguable. It is pointless, for instance, to argue that a particular Web site is a "good Web site." As a Y term, "good Web site" is broad and meaningless. Narrow down your Y term so that it is broad enough to be an interesting and recognizable category but small enough to be manageable.

You should use research to support not only your evaluative claim but also your criteria. What makes a personal home page especially effective? What makes an online movie database user-friendly? Find out what other people have said. Consult other similar sites and examine their components.

TOPIC PROPOSAL

Your topic proposal should state your evaluative claim, list your evaluative criteria as you understand them now, and explain how you will persuade readers that these criteria are indeed a legitimate measure of your Y term. The topic proposal should be one paragraph long and carefully proofread.

Proposal Argument

We strongly recommend the rhetorical analysis as the first essay in your course. Similarly, we strongly recommend the proposal argument as the final essay. Proposals require students to engage with the world in which they live, and like no other kind of essay, they require students to examine the needs and beliefs of their target audience. After all, in a proposal you are not only attempting to persuade your audience to consider your own views. You are attempting to move them to action, and as we all know, people are generally more inclined to keep things the same than they are to change.

This essay is especially challenging for teachers and students because students often find, as they begin their work, that the problem they have chosen to address is much more complicated than they initially expected. As with the definitional argument, we recommend that you be especially vigilant while students are in the early parts of their projects. Make sure they know the scope of their proposals, and point them in the right direction as best you can. The more you help them early on, the less likely you are to read a final draft in which a student proposes that your school simply "build more parking lots" or "open a greengrocery on campus" without any consideration of the complications and costs that such plans entail.

As directed in Chapter 13, each student should choose a proposal that they can handle effectively in a five-page paper. Encourage them to think small, crafting a proposal based on their own experience.

We find this an especially rewarding assignment. Many students work up a great deal of enthusiasm as they pursue their work. They interview their classmates and fellow dorm residents; they meet with campus administrators and deans; they talk with local merchants and officials and, perhaps for the first time, think of themselves as citizens of a larger community—one in which rules and regulations are necessary but also open to reconsideration.

Model Assignment Sheet: Proposal Argument

Using the principles of argumentation outlined in Part 1 of *Good Reasons with Contemporary Arguments*, choose a problem that is important or interesting to you and propose a solution to it. Your proposal may use this formula:

> We should (or should not) do **X** because. . .

Your proposal should include the following elements:

- A claim that makes a proposal that is specific and appropriate to the audience you are addressing

- An appropriate explanation of both the problem and the significance of your proposal

- Statements that clearly relate the proposal claim to the problem or need

- Evidence that the proposal will effectively address the need or solve the problem, and that it is feasible

- A consideration of alternative proposals and conditions for rebuttal

Your paper should be three to five pages long, typed, double-spaced, and carefully proofread. You should use MLA (or APA) guidelines for formatting and include a Works Cited page.

GRADING CRITERIA

I will evaluate your essay according to these criteria:

- Careful exposition of your argument's significance

- Demonstrated understanding of proposals as explained in *Good Reasons*, Chapter 13

- Acknowledgement and consideration of alternative claims and conditions for rebuttal

- Thorough consideration of your audience and effective employment of strategies designed to persuade them

- Effective essay structure

- Effective use, citation, and documentation of source material

- Clear and precise sentence-level rhetoric (grammar and style)

- Adherence to MLA (or APA) formatting guidelines, as presented in *Good Reasons with Contemporary Arguments*, Chapters 20–21

TIPS AND REMINDERS

Review the "Steps to Proposal Argument" in *Good Reasons with Contemporary Arguments*, Chapter 13.

Think small! Don't propose changes to the national health care system. However, you might consider proposing a change to the appointment system at your local doctor's office. The smaller your issue, the more manageable it will be. Consider problems in your dorm, in your high school, in your hometown, or in your place of work.

Use your own research (interviews, surveys, graphs, polls) and, if necessary, library research. This research can show that there are other problems like yours in the world and that people are concerned about them.

Find an appropriate audience for your proposal. Who can implement your suggestions for change, or who is charged with considering possible solutions to the problem you have described? You need to write to someone who will be able to enact or perhaps vote on your proposal.

Be detailed in your description of how the solution will work: how much money will it cost? Who will be responsible for implementing it? How easily can it be implemented? How much time will it take to implement your plan and make it work? What kinds of materials and labor are needed to make it work? The details you omit may be the ones that will leave the audience in doubt of your proposal's feasibility and your credibility.

In your conclusion, be sure to state your case clearly and directly so that your audience feels as if they should act on the problem you have outlined, preferably in the way you propose.

TOPIC PROPOSAL

Answer the following questions as your topic proposal:

- Describe the problem you've chosen to address.

- What is your proposal?

- Who is your audience? Why have you chosen this audience? What power do they have to enact this proposal?

- How will you make this argument so that it appeals to this particular audience?

- What kinds of research do you plan to do in writing this proposal?

- What problems do you foresee in writing this essay?

Peer Review

Peer review is an important part of the writing process. It introduces your students to their peers' writing and, over the course of the term, helps them learn to critique other writers' arguments as well as revise their own. We generally have our students complete a peer review with each of their major essays.

Students often think that a "peer review" means a session in micro-editing or proofreading. It's important to discuss with your class the goals of a peer review, and to connect this discussion to your more general discussions of the writing process. The student may still be experimenting with certain claims and reasons; his or her research is likely not yet complete; the essay's structure might still be provisional. It's also possible that some students will not have addressed the central questions of the assignment, and that their first drafts are rougher than you would like them to be. Talk with your students about what they ought to do as peer reviewers in each of these situations. And continue to talk with them about peer reviews throughout the term. By the end of the course, they should know that, before commenting on a draft, they should assess where the writer is in the process of composition. Is this essay really ready for line editing? Or is the writer still struggling to formulate a claim and good reasons? In short, they should know that a peer reviewer first needs to have a clear sense of the nature of the draft before her or him. Only then can she or he offer the writer effective assistance.

The model handouts that follow offer one way of conducting peer reviews through the term. The first handout (for the rhetorical analysis) describes the first peer review assignment of the term. Thus, it offers very specific instructions for in-class work and gives students a sense of what they should be looking for. The second handout (for the proposal argument) shows how you might conduct the final peer review of the term. The sheet is much less prescriptive, explaining to students that they need to use their own developing sense of judgment to generate questions and observations about their partners' drafts.

If you choose to hold peer review sessions in class, think about your particular class and how you can most effectively pair or group them. We have used groups of two and three (but rarely more than that) and have had success with both. We have also used various means of sorting students, sometimes doing it randomly, sometimes making the groups up beforehand, sometimes letting students choose their own partners. Decide what will work best for your class.

Some teachers assign peer review homework assignments after an in-class peer review. Generally this involves having each student take home a peer's essay. Before the next class, the student might answer a set of detailed questions about the essay: what is this essay's central argument? Describe the ethos of the writer. How might this writer revise this essay so that it more effectively "connects" with its target audience? Answering these questions, the peer reviewer serves both as a critic and a sort of mirror for the writer, showing both where the writer needs to improve and how the writer and argument appear to other readers. An alternative homework assignment requires a peer reviewer to write a one- or two-page letter to the writer, *arguing* either that the draft is ineffective or that it is effective but needs certain revisions. This type of assignment makes the peer reviewer construct a mini-essay in which his or her audience and purpose are clear. The reviewer's task is to persuade the essay writer—using claims, good reasons, and specific evidence—of a certain plan for revision.

We generally don't assign grades to peer reviews, or if we do, we do so in the most general way, using checks, check minuses, and check plusses. We are mainly concerned that students take these assignments seriously. Often you can accomplish that by reading the peer reviews and commenting on both the quality of the advice and the ethos of the peer reviewers. Your comments can be those of an interested observer: "Gosh, that's harsh!" or "That's especially good advice. I agree."

Model Peer Review Procedures:
Rhetorical Analysis

You will have this one class day for group work on your essays. Divide the time equally among your group members. Distribute copies of the paper and begin quickly. Your in-class time should be for discussion. You will complete a written response for homework.

FOR THE GROUPS

1. Begin by having each writer explain in 2–3 minutes the general argument of his or her essay: What is the argumentative aim of the chosen article? What is its central claim? Who is its audience? What is the central claim of the writer's essay?
2. Now swap essays. Before you begin reading each essay, read through these instructions so that you'll know what to look for as you read.
3. When reading, mark those places that you'll need to return to when answering the questions below. You should also mark those places that you want to discuss further with the writer. Remember: you will not have read the article that the writer has chosen. However, while reading the essay, you should be given a clear sense of the article's argument, its intended audience, and the way it attempts to persuade its readers. If, after reading the essay, you don't have a clear sense of these things, *tell the writer.* He or she will need to address this problem in the revision.
4. Once everyone has read every draft, talk about each in turn. It may be awkward at first to get discussion started, but don't worry. You might begin by noting all the things that the writer did well.
5. In your discussion, address general issues first:
   - Do you get a clear sense of the article from the essay? That is, after reading this essay, could you summarize the argument of the article and its general rhetorical strategy?

174

- Does the essay assess the structure, language, and style of the argument?
- Does the essay address ethos, pathos, and logos? Does the writer clearly present how each of the rhetorical appeals functions (or does not function) in the article?
- Has the writer completed the assignment? Does the essay, in its introductory paragraph, identify the central claim of the article and its intended audience? Has the writer assessed the overall effectiveness of the article's argument?

6. Point out the places in the writer's paper that you found effective and places that you think could use improvement. Feel free to ask the writer questions. Maybe you want the writer to clarify his or her intentions in a certain paragraph, or to find out why he or she made certain choices about the paper. Offer suggestions for improvement. Does the introductory paragraph have a thesis? Is the organization of the paper effective? Does the essay focus on those factors most significant in the article's success or lack thereof? Are there places where grammar, clarity, or format confuse readers or slow them down?

7. Elaborate on one another's responses and encourage everyone to contribute. Discussion should be among all three people in the group.

8. When you make suggestions, be sure to point to specific places in the paper. Make your advice as detailed as you can.

9. Be sensitive to the feelings of the writer, but also be honest. The best groups are supportive and critical of each paper.

FOR THE WRITER

10. Take notes on your group members' responses. Don't trust your memory!

11. Take your group members' comments seriously, but don't feel obligated to make every change they suggest. The paper is ultimately yours, and it should reflect your choices about what's most effective. If you want a second (or third) opinion, check with me.

12. Listen to your group members and ask them questions. Require them to be specific in their comments. Ask them to elaborate when you're not entirely sure what they mean.

Model Peer Review Procedures:
Proposal Argument

By now, you know how to conduct a peer review, so I have not offered you explicit instructions for this peer review session. This time, the responsibility for the discussion is yours. As trained critical readers, you need to read carefully and generate your own observations and suggestions regarding how your partners should revise their first drafts.

SUGGESTIONS FOR DISCUSSION

- Who is the writer's audience? Is the essay crafted so that it will appeal to this particular audience?

- Is the writer's ethos strong from the start? Evaluate the writer's ethos as you read. Ask yourself if the writer demonstrates the proper authority on or enough knowledge of the given topic? Why should the audience consider this writer's arguments? Has the writer "done his or her homework"? Does he or she need to do some more research?

- What is the problem that this proposal is meant to address? Is the problem adequately described?

- What is the proposal? Will the audience consider this a feasible proposal? Does this proposal clearly address the problem?

- What are the writer's reasons? Are these reasons effectively supported? Are these reasons good reasons?

- Has the writer considered other proposals and potential solutions to this problem?

- Are there places where the writer might consider reorganization?

Revision Record

We often have our students turn in a revision record along with a final draft of an essay. Here they record the work they did in rethinking, revising, editing, and proofreading their first drafts. The exercise is helpful for a number of reasons. It requires students to consider the kinds of changes they make when revising. Do they tend to sweat the small stuff and ignore major problems? Do they forget to proofread? Revision records often help students get a better sense of their own habits of revision. This assignment can also improve the quality of the revision process. Many students have told us that they revised more deliberately because of the revision record assignment. Knowing that they had to record the work they did, they went about it with more care.

We have also found it helpful to have revision records before us when grading. Reading through one of these assignments, you can quickly get a sense of a student's habits of revision. The records also provide an effective starting point in student conferences.

If you are using a composition or grammar handbook in your course, see if it includes a section on revising, editing, and proofreading. If so, consider incorporating the language of that text into the revision record. Some texts, for instance, differentiate between "revising," "editing," and "proofreading" (we have used such a scheme here). By incorporating your grammar text into the work of the course, you encourage students to use the text regularly.

Finally, we recommend that you keep the revision record a simple assignment. Complicated revision records are often unsuccessful; students do not complete them with the same care and attention. In fact, it seems that complicated revision record assignments actually discourage the kind of work they are meant to encourage!

Model Revision Record Assignment

With your final draft, you will turn in a one- or two-sheet record of what exactly you did in revising your essay. Your revision record should have three sections: revision, editing, and proofreading. You should classify the work you did after completing your first draft accordingly.

- Under "Revision," include the global or large-scale changes you made. Did you refine the focus of the essay? Did you somehow revise your rhetorical purpose, or narrow or change your target audience? Did you change the structure of your essay, modify its central argument, or provide further evidence to support your claim and reasons?

- Under "Editing," include small-scale changes. Did you make your language more concrete? Did you work to make your transitions from paragraph to paragraph more effective? Did you polish the opening and closing paragraphs so that they fit your revised argument exactly?

- Under "Proofreading," include those final changes that often greatly affect the impression an essay makes, even with teachers. Did you run the spell-check program on your word processor? Did you check one last time those areas in which you know you need work? Did you check the punctuation of the essay and correct any typographical errors? Did you check the essay's formatting?

Be as complete as you can when writing this record. Note all the changes you made. You might even write the record over a series of several days as you revise your essay.

Your revision record will be of great help when I read your final draft. We will also use it when we meet to discuss your work on the essay.

Self-Assessment

When students turn in a major essay—one that they have drafted several times and thought about for several weeks—they often want to do more than simply hand it over and begin the next unit. Therefore, we often have our students write self-assessments on the day a major essay is due. This does not need to be an especially demanding assignment. In fact, like the revision record, we find that students provide more meaningful comments if they see it as something not particularly taxing. Several times, much to our surprise, we have assigned brief self-assessment assignments that students took 20–25 minutes to complete.

This sort of assignment is beneficial in so many ways: it offers students a final say regarding their essays; it allows them to articulate what they think is strong, and not so strong, in the work they give to you; and, along with the revision record, it provides you a sense of the student's estimation of his or her own work.

Last, these assignments also give you a sense of the class as a whole. The similarities in a stack of self-assessments are often striking. You see what the students have not yet absorbed as a class. You also see a reflection of your own teaching in the unit—those concepts, strategies, and conventions that you emphasized, and those you did not. The assignments are fascinating reading, and we encourage you to read through them as soon as you can. Often, we select especially interesting, significant, or provocative excerpts from the responses and show them to the class at our next meeting. This can be a simple and effective way of revealing to students that their experiences in your class—their frustration with a definition argument, say, or their developing confidence as a critical reader—are often shared by their classmates. These comments also often provide nice segues from one unit to the next.

Model Self-Assessment Assignment: Essay One

Congratulations! You have finished your first essay. Before turning in your work, take the next ten minutes to answer the following questions. As in your peer review and revision record, be as specific in your responses as you can.

1. First, consider your final draft. In what ways is it especially strong?
2. What parts of this essay, in your opinion, still need work?
3. Now, think back over the work you did for this essay—writing the topic proposal, putting the first draft together, revising the first draft, polishing the final draft, and so on. At what stage in this process did you do especially good work? What do you plan to do differently in your work on the second essay?

Model Syllabi

Using *Good Reasons with Contemporary Arguments*, we have created two model syllabi: one emphasizes kinds of arguments; the other emphasizes the forums in which arguments are often made. Both syllabi are designed to cover research skills and documentation, visual design, and oral presentations. Also, both are constructed to allow you to move through the writing process (i.e., from topic proposal to final draft) in each formal essay assignment.

These are not generic syllabi. We have made a number of choices in constructing them—choices, for instance, about the kinds of essays assigned, the order in which the class moves through *Good Reasons with Contemporary Arguments*, and the emphasis of the assignments. Before designing your course, decide how you want to teach the material covered in *Good Reasons with Contemporary Arguments* in order to meet both your own and your home institution's goals.

Finally, we did not create these syllabi because we think that they constitute the best or only way to teach a course in argumentation. Rather, our goal is to provide you with several models that grow out of the pedagogical philosophy in which *Good Reasons with Contemporary Arguments* is grounded. Of course, we also want to provide you with realistic, specific, and serviceable models in planning your own class.

Syllabus 1: Emphasis on Kinds of Argument

This syllabus emphasizes different kinds of arguments. It also focuses on the skills necessary for effective writing, research, and documentation.

FEATURES

- This course covers all of *Good Reasons with Contemporary Arguments* and constitutes a rigorous introduction to the different kinds of arguments presented in the text.

- The syllabus allows you either to provide students with common topics for their formal essays, or to allow them to choose their own topics.

- The syllabus is designed to allow you enough time to move completely through the writing process with each of the four formal assignments.

- Research skills are introduced in the second unit and may then be reviewed in the third and fourth units.

- The fundamentals of visual and Web design are introduced in the third unit and may be reviewed in the fourth.

- Oral presentations are covered in the fourth unit.

SCOPE

This course offers a rigorous introduction to the different kinds of arguments presented in *Good Reasons with Contemporary Arguments*. The first unit addresses basic rhetorical concepts, including arguability, the rhetorical appeals, and the nature of an audience-centered arguments. The first unit also addresses the writing process, and students are asked to consider effective strategies not only for writing but also for invention and revision. The following units build on the first. Students complete formal assignments that vary according to the kind of argument (rather than forum in which the argument is being made). The course culminates with a proposal argument in which students write an extended essay (or possibly design a Web site) advocating for a specific change in their community.

UNIT ONE: ARGUMENTS AND GOOD REASONS

Coverage

- Subject and goals of the course
- Policy statement and syllabus
- The definition and basics of argument
- Audience-centered approaches to argumentation
- The writing process and its place in the course
- Critical reading

Readings

- Chapter 1, "Why Argue?"
- Chapter 2, "Reading Arguments"
- Chapter 3, "Finding Arguments"
- Chapter 5, "Analyzing Written Arguments"
- Chapter 6, "Analyzing Visual Arguments"
- Chapter 4, "Drafting and Revising Arguments"

Contemporary Arguments

- You have several options here. You might choose to read all the arguments clustered around a central topic, such as the arguments addressing immigration. That way, while addressing the central rhetorical concepts of the course, you and your students can examine many of the claims made in the debates over a single issue. You can practice classifying claims as definitional, causal, evaluative, or proposal, identifying the genres of argument (e.g., rebuttal, narrative, visual), and identifying how each writer shapes his or her work for a particular audience.

- Alternatively, you might read arguments from several or all of the topic clusters, choosing those that seem most accessible to students in the first weeks of the course. By choosing this option, you introduce some variety into your readings and preview many of the issues that you'll address throughout the semester. One set of essays for this option involves the following:

Additional Readings

- Issue in Focus: Biometrics and Measuring the Body for Identity (Ch. 26) to go along with Ch. 1

- Merkle, "Nanotechnology: Designs for the Future" (Ch. 25) to go along with Ch. 2

- Bérubé, "Citizenship and Disability" and Udovitch, "A Secret Society of the Starving" (Ch. 27) to go along with Ch. 3

- Vasque, "Appearances" and Haeringer, "Coming Out in the Line of Fire" (Ch. 23) to go along with Ch. 5

- American Legacy Foundation, Antismoking Ad, Trudeau, "Doonesbury," and Morris, Camel Lights Ad (all Ch. 27) to go along with Ch. 6

- Issue in Focus: Stem Cell Research (Ch. 25) to go along with Ch. 4

In-Class Activities and Short Assignments

- Discuss the meanings of "argument" and "rhetoric" (Chs. 1–2).

- List arguments encountered in a single day (Ch. 1).

- Work in groups and prepare a draft argument that includes all four parts of a model argument (Ch. 2).

- Assess *sufficient* and *relevant* evidence (Ch. 3).
- Identify logical fallacies in arguments (Ch. 3).
- Write a brief rhetorical textual analysis (Ch. 5).
- Write a brief rhetorical contextual analysis (Ch. 5).
- Discuss sample visual arguments (Ch. 6).
- Make a plan for revision (Ch. 4).

Formal Assignments

- Write an extended, textual rhetorical analysis of a persuasive text
- Write an extended, contextual rhetorical analysis of a persuasive text

UNIT TWO: DEFINITION ARGUMENTS, CAUSAL ARGUMENTS, EFFECTIVE RESEARCH

Coverage

- Definition and causal arguments
- Effective research skills
- Locating, assessing, and using print and electronic sources
- Summarizing, paraphrasing, and quoting effectively
- Scholastic honesty and effective documentation

Readings

- Chapter 8, "Definition Arguments"
- Chapter 9, "Causal Arguments"
- Chapter 16, "Planning Research"

- Chapter 17, "Finding Sources"

- Chapter 18, "Evaluating and Recording Sources"

- Chapter 20, "MLA Documentation" or

- Chapter 21, "APA Documentation"

Contemporary Arguments

- For a list of the definitional and causal arguments that appear in *Good Reasons with Contemporary Arguments*, consult the Alternate Table of Contents in the front matter of the text.

- For a list of the arguments appearing in *Good Reasons with Contemporary Arguments* that cite sources, consult the Alternate Table of Contents in the front matter of the text.

- Instead of reading definitional and causal arguments on various issues, you might choose to read all the arguments clustered around one topic. In doing so, you will cover some arguments that aren't *primarily* definitional or causal. Nevertheless, you and your students can examine how certain terms and causal chains are central to any debate, even in arguments in which they aren't the primary concern.

Additional Readings

- Definition Arguments: Hackbarth, "Vanity, Thy Name Is Metrosexual" (Ch. 23); Ngai, "No Human Being is Illegal" and Deardorff, "In Search of Intercultural Competence" (Ch. 24)

- Causal Arguments: Sullivan, "The End of Gay Culture" (Ch. 23); Malkin, "Beware of Illegal Aliens Seeking Hazmat Licenses" (Ch. 24); Larsen, "Traveler's Card Might Just Pave the Way for a National ID Card" (Ch. 26)

- Documentation: Bettcher and Subramaniam, "The Necessity of Global Tobacco Regulation" (Ch. 27); Boyd, "Facebook's Privacy Trainwreck: Exposure, Invasion, and Social Convergence" (Ch. 28)

In-Class Activities and Short Assignments

- Generate a list of X and Y terms for definition arguments (Ch. 8).

- Discuss the causal methods of common factor, single difference, concomitant variation, and process of elimination (Ch. 9).

- Discuss the causes for a particular phenomenon (Ch. 9).

- Visit the campus library (Ch. 16).

- Assess different kinds of sources (e.g., print and online, popular, trade, and scholarly journals) (Ch. 17).

- Develop a worksheet to assess print and online sources (Ch. 18).

- Answer the questions listed under "Research: Knowing What Information You Need" (Ch. 17).

- Compile an annotated list of the online sources available at your home institution (Ch. 17).

- Discuss "common knowledge" as opposed to information that needs to be documented (Ch. 19).

- Paraphrase an editorial or scholarly article (Ch. 19).

- Interview an older student about sources and documentation (Ch. 15).

Formal Assignments

- Write a definition argument

- Write a causal argument

UNIT THREE: EVALUATION ARGUMENTS, NARRATIVE ARGUMENTS, REBUTTAL ARGUMENTS, EFFECTIVE DESIGN

Coverage

- Evaluation, narrative, and rebuttal arguments
- The rhetoric of print and visual design
- The nature of arguments in electronic environments

Readings

- Chapter 10, "Evaluation Arguments"
- Chapter 11, "Narrative Arguments"
- Chapter 12, "Rebuttal Arguments"
- Chapter 14, "Designing Arguments"

Contemporary Arguments

- For a list of the evaluation, narrative, and rebuttal arguments that appear in *Good Reasons with Contemporary Arguments*, consult the Alternate Table of Contents in the front matter of the text.

- For a list of the visual arguments appearing in *Good Reasons with Contemporary Arguments*, consult the Alternate Table of Contents in the front matter of the text.

- Again, instead of reading arguments on various issues, you might choose to read all the arguments clustered around one topic. In doing so, you will cover some arguments that aren't *primarily* evaluative, narrative, or designed to rebut some other argument. Nevertheless, you and your students can examine how evaluation, narration, and rebuttal are central to any debate, even in arguments in which they aren't the primary concern.

- Evaluation Arguments: Joy, "Why the Future Doesn't Need Us" and Fukuyama, "A Tale of Two Dystopias" (Ch. 25); Brin, "Three Cheers for the Surveillance Society" (Ch. 26)

- Narrative Arguments: Momaday, "The Way to Rainy Mountain" and Walker, "Am I Blue?" (Ch. 22)

- Rebuttal: Issue in Focus: Stem Cell Research (Ch. 25); Califano, "The Right Drug to Target" and Schlosser, "Make Peace with Pot" (Ch. 27)

In-Class Activities and Short Assignments

- Conduct an in-class "Best of. . ." poll and determine the criteria used in evaluating certain products, or facilities (Ch. 10).

- Discuss the differences among and between aesthetic, practical, and moral criteria (Ch. 10).

- Write two very brief narrations of an experience. Write the first from a positive perspective; write the second from a negative perspective (Ch. 11).

- Discuss effective and ineffective uses of personal narrative and humor in argument (Ch. 11).

- Analyze an advertisement that consists mostly of visual content (Ch. 14).

- Examine texts with misleading visual elements (Ch. 14).

- Redesign a document or Web site that has poor visual design (Ch. 14).

- Create a resume (Ch. 14).

- Perform a rhetorical analysis of a particular CD's packaging (Ch. 14).

- Organize and present a copious amount of data effectively (Ch. 14).

Formal Assignments

- Evaluate a Web site for a particular audience or publication (Ch. 14).

- Write a narrative argument (Ch. 11). Consider giving your students a specific rhetorical situation for this assignment. For instance, several publications include narrative arguments written by readers (NPR's "This I Believe" features, for example). You might have students write this assignment according to a magazine's submission guidelines.

- Write a rebuttal to an argument (Ch. 12).

- Design a Web site that makes an effective evaluation, narrative, or rebuttal argument.

UNIT FOUR: PROPOSAL ARGUMENTS, ORAL PRESENTATIONS

Coverage

- Proposal arguments
- Oral presentations
- Review of the kinds of arguments
- Review of what's involved in writing for a particular audience
- Review of effective research skills and the use, assessment, and documentation of sources
- Review of the writing process, peer revision, and editing

Readings

- Chapter 13, "Proposal Arguments"
- Chapter 15, "Presenting Arguments"

Contemporary Arguments

- For a list of the proposal arguments that appear in *Good Reasons with Contemporary Arguments*, consult the Alternate Table of Contents in the front matter of the text.

- For a list of the arguments appearing in *Good Reasons with Contemporary Arguments* that cite sources, consult the Alternate Table of Contents in the front matter of the text.

- Instead of reading proposal arguments on various issues, you might choose to read all the arguments clustered around one topic. In doing so, you will cover some arguments that aren't *primarily* proposals. Nevertheless, you and your students can examine how proposals build upon other kinds of claims.

Additional Readings

- Proposal Arguments: House of Representatives, The Defense of Marriage Act (Ch. 23); Bettcher and Subramaniam, "The Necessity of Global Tobacco Regulations" and Rafferty, "Kate Winslet, Please Save Us!" (Ch. 27)

In-Class Activities and Short Assignments

- Propose some solutions for actions or things that "tick you off" (Ch. 13).

- Generate a list of problems around town or campus that need to be addressed (Ch. 13).

- Write a proposal argument as a class (Ch. 13).

- Create presentations with effective time-management and focus (Ch. 15).

- Create a presentation from a past paper (Ch. 15).

Formal Assignments

- Write an extended proposal argument in which students advocate for a specific change or course of action.

- Develop an oral or multimedia presentation advocating for a specific change or course of action.

Syllabus 2: Emphasis on Forums for Arguments

This syllabus emphasizes not claim types but the different forums or spaces in which people make arguments. It also covers the skills necessary for effective writing, research, and documentation.

FEATURES

- This course covers all of *Good Reasons with Contemporary Arguments* and focuses on the variety of forums (e.g., personal narratives, editorials, position papers, Web sites, oral presentations) in which people make arguments.

- The course also emphasizes research. Research skills are introduced in the second unit, then covered comprehensively in the third.

- The syllabus allows you either to provide students with common topics for their formal essays, or to allow students to choose their own topics.

- The syllabus is designed to allow you enough time to move completely through the writing process with each of the four formal assignments.

- Oral presentations and the fundamentals of visual and Web design are covered in the fourth unit.

SCOPE

This course introduces students to the different forums for arguments. The first unit uses narrative arguments to introduce students to basic rhetorical concepts, including arguability, the three rhetorical appeals, and the nature of audience-centered arguments. The first unit also addresses the writing process, and students are asked to consider effective strategies not only for writing but also for invention and revision. In following units, students address the other forums for argument, assessing the rhetorical strategies and conventions particular to each. The course culminates with an assignment in which students make a persuasive argument in the form of a Web site, an oral presentation, or a visual display.

UNIT ONE: PERSONAL NARRATIVE

Coverage

- Subject and goals of the course
- Narrative arguments
- The definition and basics of argument
- Audience-centered approaches to argumentation
- The writing process and its place in the course
- Critical reading

Readings

- Chapter 1, "Why Argue?"
- Chapter 2, "Reading Arguments"
- Chapter 3, "Finding Arguments"
- Chapter 4, "Drafting and Revising Arguments"
- Chapter 5, "Analyzing Written Arguments"
- Chapter 11, "Narrative Arguments"

Contemporary Arguments

- For a list of the narrative arguments that appear in *Good Reasons with Contemporary Arguments*, consult the Alternate Table of Contents in the front matter of the text.

- Issue in Focus: Biometrics and Measuring the Body for Identity (Ch. 26) to go along with Ch. 1

- Merkle, "Nanotechnology: Designs for the Future" (Ch. 25) to go along with Ch. 2

- Bérubé, "Citizenship and Disability" and Udovitch, "A Secret Society of the Starving" (Ch. 27) to go along with Ch. 3

- Issue in Focus: Stem Cell Research (Ch. 25) to go along with Ch. 4

- Vasque, "Appearances" and Haeringer, "Coming Out in the Line of Fire" (Ch. 23) to go along with Ch. 5

- Narrative Arguments: Momaday, "The Way to Rainy Mountain" and Walker, "Am I Blue?" (Ch. 22)

Contemporary Arguments

- For a list of the definition, causal, evaluation, and rebuttal arguments that appear in *Good Reasons with Contemporary Arguments*, consult the Alternate Table of Contents in the front matter of the text.

- Instead of reading arguments on various issues, you might choose to read all the arguments clustered around one topic. In doing so, you and your students can examine how definition, evaluation, causal, and rebuttal are central to any debate, even in arguments in which they aren't the primary concern.

Additional Readings

- Definition Arguments: Hackbarth, "Vanity, Thy Name Is Metrosexual" (Ch. 23); Ngai, "No Human Being is Illegal" and Deardorff, "In Search of Intercultural Competence" (Ch. 24)

- Causal Arguments: Sullivan, "The End of Gay Culture" (Ch. 23); Malkin, "Beware of Illegal Aliens Seeking Hazmat Licenses" (Ch. 24); Larsen, "Traveler's Card Might Just Pave the Way for a National ID Card" (Ch. 26)

- Evaluation Arguments: Joy, "Why the Future Doesn't Need Us" and Fukuyama, "A Tale of Two Dystopias" (Ch. 25); Brin, "Three Cheers for the Surveillance Society" (Ch. 26)

- Rebuttal: Issue in Focus: Stem Cell Research (Ch. 25); Califano, "The Right Drug to Target" and Schlosser, "Make Peace with Pot" (Ch. 27)

In-Class Activities and Short Assignments

- Discuss the meanings of "argument" and "rhetoric" (Chs. 1–2).

- List arguments encountered in a single day (Ch. 1).

- Work in groups and prepare a draft argument that includes all four parts of a model argument (Ch. 2).

- Assess *sufficient* and *relevant* evidence (Ch. 3).

- Identify logical fallacies in arguments (Ch. 3).

- Rewrite an argument for a different audience (Ch. 4).

- Describe a memory from both positive and negative perspectives (Ch. 11).

- Discuss effective and ineffective uses of personal narrative and humor in argument (Ch. 11).

- Make a plan for revision (Ch. 4).

Formal Assignments

- Write a narrative argument (Ch. 11). Consider giving your students a specific rhetorical situation for this assignment. For instance, several publications include narrative arguments written by readers (NPR's "This I Believe" features, for example). You might have students write this assignment according to a magazine's submission guidelines.

- Analyze the rhetorical appeals used in a narrative argument.

UNIT TWO: KINDS OF ARGUMENTS

Coverage

- Definition, causal, evaluation, and rebuttal arguments
- Introduction to research skills
- Summarizing, paraphrasing, and quoting
- Scholastic honesty
- Introduction to effective documentation

Readings

- Chapter 8, "Definition Arguments"
- Chapter 9, "Causal Arguments"
- Chapter 10, "Evaluation Arguments"
- Chapter 12, "Rebuttal Arguments"
- Chapter 20, "MLA Documentation" or
- Chapter 21, "APA Documentation"

In-Class Activities and Short Assignments

- Generate a list of X and Y terms for definitional arguments (Ch. 8).
- Discuss the causal methods of common factor, single difference, concomitant variation, and process of elimination (Ch. 9).
- Discuss the causes for a particular phenomenon (Ch. 9).
- Analyze a causal argument that uses graphic or visual evidence (Ch. 9).

- Conduct an in-class "Best of . . ." poll and determine the criteria used in evaluating the results (Ch. 10).

- Discuss the differences among and between aesthetic, practical, and moral criteria (Ch. 10).

Formal Assignments

- Write an editorial addressing a particular local or national issue.

- Review a restaurant, movie, television show, performance, or local band for a general-audience entertainment magazine or newspaper.

UNIT THREE: EFFECTIVE RESEARCH

Coverage

- Proposal Arguments
- Continuation of research and documentation
- Continuation of summarizing, paraphrasing, and quoting
- Continuation of scholastic honesty

Readings

- Chapter 13, "Proposal Arguments"
- Chapter 16, "Planning Research"
- Chapter 17, "Finding Sources"
- Chapter 18, "Evaluating and Recording Sources"
- Chapter 19, "Writing the Research Paper"
- Chapter 20, "MLA Documentation" or
- Chapter 21, "APA Documentation"

Contemporary Arguments

- For a list of the arguments appearing in *Good Reasons with Contemporary Arguments* that cite sources, consult the Alternate Table of Contents in the front matter of the text.

- Instead of reading proposal arguments on various issues, you might choose to read all the arguments clustered around one topic. This fits particularly well with a focus on forums rather than types of arguments. In doing so, you will cover some arguments that aren't *primarily* proposals. Nevertheless, you and your students can examine how proposals build upon other kinds of claims.

Additional Readings

- Proposal Arguments: House of Representatives, The Defense of Marriage Act (Ch. 23); Bettcher and Subramaniam, "The Necessity of Global Tobacco Regulations" and Rafferty, "Kate Winslet, Please Save Us!" (Ch. 27)

- Documentation: Bettcher and Subramaniam, "The Necessity of Global Tobacco Regulation" (Ch. 27); Boyd, "Facebook's Privacy Trainwreck: Exposure, Invasion, and Social Convergence" (Ch. 28)

In-Class Activities and Short Assignments

- Generate a list of problems around town or campus that need to be addressed (Ch. 13).

- Write a proposal argument as a class (Ch. 13).

- Compile an annotated list of the online sources available at your home institution (Ch. 16)

- Visit the campus library (Ch. 16).

- Assess different kinds of sources (e.g., print and online, popular, trade, and scholarly journals) (Ch. 17).

- Develop a worksheet to assess print and online sources (Ch. 18).
- Answer the questions listed under "Research: Knowing What Information You Need" (Ch. 17).
- Discuss "common knowledge" as opposed to information that needs to be documented (Ch. 19).
- Paraphrase a persuasive piece of writing (Ch. 19).
- Interview an older student about sources and documentation (Ch. 15).

Formal Assignments

- Research and write an academic argument. This paper can take many forms, of course. You might allow students to choose their own topics, perhaps encouraging them to find something in their field of study.

UNIT FOUR: VISUAL AND ORAL PRESENTATIONS

Coverage

- Visual Design
- Web Design
- Oral Presentations
- Continuation of research and documentation
- Continuation of summarizing, paraphrasing, and quoting
- Continuation of scholastic honesty

Readings

- Chapter 6, "Analyzing Visual Arguments"

- Chapter 14, "Designing Arguments"

- Chapter 15, "Presenting Arguments"

Contemporary Arguments

- For a list of the visual arguments appearing in *Good Reasons with Contemporary Arguments*, consult the Alternate Table of Contents in the front matter of the text.

Additional Readings

- Visual Arguments: American Legacy Foundation, Antismoking Ad, Trudeau, "Doonesbury," and Morris, Camel Lights Ad (all Ch. 27) to go along with Ch. 6

In-Class Activities and Short Assignments

- Perform rhetorical analyses on advertisements that rely on visual arguments (Ch. 6).

- Examine texts with misleading visual elements (Ch. 14).

- Redesign a document or Web site that has poor visual design (Ch. 15).

- Create a resume (Ch. 14).

- Perform a rhetorical analysis of a particular CD's packaging (Ch. 14).

- Organize and present a copious amount of data effectively (Ch. 14).

- Create presentations with effective time-management and focus (Ch. 15).

- Create a presentation from a past paper (Ch. 15).

Formal Assignments

- Design an ad campaign for a particular product, institution, or issue.

- Create an effectively designed Web site or brochure advocating a cause.

- Deliver a focused, effective oral presentation (IM, pp. 58–60).